# VMware vCenter Operations Manager Essentials

Explore virtualization fundamentals and real-world solutions for the modern network administrator

**Lauren Malhoit**

[PACKT] enterprise

PUBLISHING    professional expertise distilled

BIRMINGHAM - MUMBAI

# VMware vCenter Operations Manager Essentials

First published: February 2014

Production Reference: 1110214

Published by Packt Publishing Ltd.
Livery Place
35 Livery Street
Birmingham B3 2PB, UK.

ISBN 978-1-78217-696-1

www.packtpub.com

Cover Image by Duraid Fatouhi (duraidfatouhi@yahoo.com)

# Credits

**Author**
Lauren Malhoit

**Reviewers**
Michael Poore
Mike Preston
Chris Wahl

**Acquisition Editors**
Ashwin Nair
Gregory Wild

**Content Development Editor**
Gregory Wild

**Technical Editors**
Mario D'Souza
Mrunmayee Patil
Aman Preet Singh

**Copy Editors**
Alisha Aranha
Sarang Chari
Gladson Monteiro

**Project Coordinator**
Venitha Cutinho

**Proofreaders**
Mario Cecere
Lindsey Thomas

**Indexers**
Hemangini Bari
Tejal Soni

**Graphics**
Yuvraj Mannari

**Production Coordinator**
Pooja Chiplunkar

**Cover Work**
Pooja Chiplunkar

# About the Author

**Lauren Malhoit** has been in the IT field for over 10 years. She's currently a technical virtualization architect specializing in virtualization and storage in the datacenter. She has been writing for TechRepublic and TechRepublic Pro for a few years as well as for `VirtualizationSoftware.com`. As a VMware vExpert, Cisco Champion, EMC Elect, and PernixPro member, Lauren tries to stay involved in the community. She also hosts a bi-weekly technology podcast called AdaptingIT (`http://www.adaptingit.com/`). Lauren has been a delegate for Tech Field Day (`http://techfieldday.com/`) several times as well.

For my mom, the wisest person I know. Without your encouragement, perseverance, and sometimes slaps in the face, I never would have made it this far! I couldn't have asked for a better role model.

# About the Reviewers

**Michael Poore** is a senior consultant for Xtravirt, a leading virtualization and cloud consultancy in the UK. Michael works primarily with enterprise customers and service providers to help solve their challenges using the VMware datacentre and cloud products along with many other related virtualization technologies. His current focus is on the design, implementation, and consumption of both private and public cloud infrastructures. In addition to being co-leader of the South West UK VMUG, Michael has also been honored for three successive years with VMware's coveted vExpert accolade. You can follow Michael Poore on Twitter (@mpoore) or his blog (http://vspecialist.co.uk).

**Mike Preston** is an IT professional, author, and an overall tech enthusiast living in Ontario, Canada. He has held all sorts of IT posts over the last 15 years including Network Technician, Systems Administrator, Programmer Analyst, Web Developer, and Systems Engineer in all sorts of different verticals, from sales to consulting. Currently, he works as a systems analyst supporting the education market near his home in Belleville, Ontario. Mike has always had an intense passion for sharing his skills, solutions, and work with various online communities, most recently focusing on virtualization communities. He is an avid blogger at blog.mwpreston. net and participates in many discussions on Twitter: @mwpreston. It's his passion for sharing within the virtualization community that has led to Mike receiving the vExpert award for 2012 and 2013. Mike has presented at VMworld, VMUGs, and various virtualization conferences on numerous occasions, both as a customer and an overall evangelist, and has published different whitepapers and articles for various tech websites. His most recent publication was *Troubleshooting vSphere Storage, Packt Publishing*, November 2013. His commitment to giving back to the community has resulted in his most recent venture of becoming a Toronto VMUG co-leader. He is a VMware Certified Professional in Datacenter Virtualization on both Versions 4 and 5 of vSphere as well as a VCAP5-DCA.

**Chris Wahl** has acquired over a decade of IT experience in enterprise infrastructure design, implementation, and administration. He has provided architectural and engineering expertise in various virtualization, data center, and private-cloud-based engagements while working with high-performance technical teams in tiered data center environments.

Chris holds well over 30 active industry certifications, including the rare VMware Certified Design Expert (VCDX #104), and is a recognized VMware vExpert. He also works to give back to the community as both an active Master user and moderator of the VMware Technology Network (VMTN) and as a leader of the Chicago VMware User Group (VMUG).

As an independent blogger for the award winning *Wahl Network*, Chris focuses on creating content that revolves around virtualization, converged infrastructure, and evangelizing products and services that benefit the technology community. Over the past several years, he has published hundreds of articles and was voted the *Favorite Independent Blogger* by vSphere-Land.com for 2012. Chris also travels globally to speak at industry events, provide subject matter expertise, and offer perspectives as a technical analyst.

# www.PacktPub.com

## Support files, eBooks, discount offers and more

You might want to visit www.PacktPub.com for support files and downloads related to your book.

Did you know that Packt offers eBook versions of every book published, with PDF and ePub files available? You can upgrade to the eBook version at www.PacktPub.com and as a print book customer, you are entitled to a discount on the eBook copy. Get in touch with us at service@packtpub.com for more details.

At www.PacktPub.com, you can also read a collection of free technical articles, sign up for a range of free newsletters and receive exclusive discounts and offers on Packt books and eBooks.

http://PacktLib.PacktPub.com

Do you need instant solutions to your IT questions? PacktLib is Packt's online digital book library. Here, you can access, read and search across Packt's entire library of books.

## Why Subscribe?

- Fully searchable across every book published by Packt
- Copy and paste, print and bookmark content
- On demand and accessible via web browser

## Free Access for Packt account holders

If you have an account with Packt at www.PacktPub.com, you can use this to access PacktLib today and view nine entirely free books. Simply use your login credentials for immediate access.

## Instant Updates on New Packt Books

Get notified! Find out when new books are published by following @PacktEnterprise on Twitter, or the *Packt Enterprise* Facebook page.

# Table of Contents

# Preface

VMware vCenter Operations Manager is a solution that allows VMware administrators to understand and troubleshoot their current and future VMware implementations. Upon initial investigation, vCenter Operations (vC Ops) seems like a fairly intuitive solution. However, with its many options for navigation and a very robust feature set, vC Ops can be slightly intimidating, especially if it's not something we use often.

*vCenter Operations Manager Administration Essentials* is a book designed to help administrators not only to install and configure vC Ops, but also learn how to use it to troubleshoot issues within the virtual environment, reclaim wasted space, understand what anomalous behavior is in their specific environment, easily monitor the VMware environment, and even produce consistent and strategic reports to help drive educated decision making within the IT department. The focus of VMware *vCenter Operations Manager Essential* is to help administrators become more comfortable with the vC Ops product and use it to its full potential.

Although this book comprehensively covers how to install and use vCenter Operations Manager, it is not meant to be a replacement for any documentation published by VMware.

## What this book covers

*Chapter 1, Introduction to vCenter Operations Manager*, provides a quick overview of how vCenter Operations (vC Ops from here on) is able to learn our environment and gives us many benefits for both troubleshooting and capacity planning.

*Chapter 2, Installing vCenter Operations Manager*, will basically be a step-by-step tutorial and with any known caveats pointed out. By the end of this chapter, we should have a full version of vC Ops running and ready to be configured.

*Chapter 3, Dashboards and Badges*, is where we really dive into vC Ops by getting familiar with the vC Ops GUI and dashboards. We learn about major and minor badges and how the different scores can affect our environment.

*Chapter 4, Troubleshooting Our Virtual Environment with vCenter Operations Manager,* is great for those of us who keep having trouble within our VMware environment. Perhaps there are some nagging issues about why we keep running out of memory resources, or maybe we have several VMs running slowly, and we'll be able to drill down and see if there's actually a problem with the data stores they're all connected to.

*Chapter 5, Capacity Planning with vCenter Operations Manager,* allows us to get into capacity planning here. We'll look at reports that will tell us whether our VMs are undersized or oversized as well as show what-if scenarios if we're looking to add more VMs to our environment. vC Ops takes out the guesswork for us.

*Chapter 6, Reports,* allows us to dive into the reports. vC Ops offers both canned reports, which can be very helpful, as well as custom reports, which can be specific to our environment. These reports are great to turn in to our director, CIO, or CTO.

*Chapter 7, vCenter Configuration Manager,* explains vCenter Configuration Manager. In this chapter, we'll go through an introduction to vCCM as well as how to install it. There will be real-life scenarios to help users understand the advantages gained when adding in compliance and change management using vCCM.

*Chapter 8, Log Insight*, explains what VMware Log Insight is and how this new product will integrate with vC Ops. It will also allow us to dive into the application and operating system to see where problems are and keep track of events. We will go through an installation of Log Insight as well as some common use cases.

*Chapter 9, VMware Horizon View Integration with vCenter Operations Manager,* will also show us how advantageous it can be to use vC Ops within our VMware View 5.2 environment. Think of all the resources VMware View uses. It would be great to be able to drill in and pinpoint that we're having a storage issue before we start messing around with all the virtual machines.

*Chapter 10, vCenter Infrastructure Navigator,* helps users to automatically discover application services and map them out within our environment. We can then hook it into vC Ops to get metrics on an entire application automatically.

*Chapter 11, EMC Storage Analytics*, explains EMC VNX SAN integration with vCenter Operations Manager. Presently we will install storage analytics on our VNX SAN, which will give us the capability to see more of what's going on in our storage environment than ever before from a VMware admin perspective.

# What you need for this book

The reader should have an understanding of VMware vSphere as well as access to a VMware vSphere environment and vCenter Operations Manager. Access to VMware vCenter Configuration Manager, VMware Horizon View, VMware Log Insight, and EMC VNX storage array are also helpful but not absolutely necessary. A knowledge of the following will also be helpful for understanding this book:

- ESXi Hosts
- VMware vCenter
- Datastores/luns
- Virtual Networking
- Light Physical Networking
- Compute (CPU, Memory) within a virtual environment

In order to implement the solutions in the book, you'll need the following:

- VMware vSphere environment with at least one host
- Datastore
- vCenter Installed
- Access to the vCenter network
- Downloaded version of vCenter Operations Manager

It would also be useful to have:

- VMware Horizon View
- vCenter Configuration Manager
- VMware Log Insight
- EMC VNX
- EMC Storage Analytics

# Who this book is for

This book is meant for administrators, engineers, and architects of VMware vSphere as well as those who are interested in purchasing vCenter Operations Manager Suite or have already purchased it. Administrators who are hoping to use vCenter Operations Manager to optimize their VMware environments as well as quickly troubleshoot both long-term and short-term issues should read this book.

# Conventions

In this book, you will find a number of styles of text that distinguish between different kinds of information. Here are some examples of these styles, and an explanation of their meaning.

Any command-line input or output is written as follows:

```
su - admin
```

URLs will appear as:

```
http://kb.vmware.com/selfservice/microsites/search.do?language=en_US&
cmd=displayKC&externalId=2046591
```

**New terms** and **important words** are shown in bold. Words that you see on the screen, in menus or dialog boxes for example, appear in the text like this: "Clicking the **Next** button moves you to the next screen."

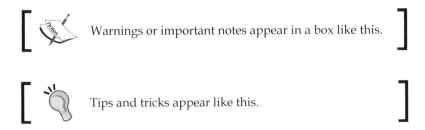

> Warnings or important notes appear in a box like this.

> Tips and tricks appear like this.

# Reader feedback

Feedback from our readers is always welcome. Let us know what you think about this book—what you liked or may have disliked. Reader feedback is important for us to develop titles that you really get the most out of.

To send us general feedback, simply send an e-mail to feedback@packtpub.com, and mention the book title via the subject of your message.

You can reach the author, Lauren Malhoit, on her site www.adaptingit.com under the Contact page as well as via her Twitter handle @Malhoit. If you are looking to read more from Lauren, she also writes for TechRepublic.com (http://www.techrepublic.com/) and SoftwareVirtualization.com.

If there is a topic that you have expertise in and you are interested in either writing or contributing to a book, see our author guide on www.packtpub.com/authors.

# Customer support

Now that you are the proud owner of a Packt book, we have a number of things to help you to get the most from your purchase.

# Downloading the color images of this book

We also provide you a PDF file that has color images of the screenshots/diagrams used in this book. The color images will help you better understand the changes in the output. You can download this file from: `https://www.packtpub.com/sites/default/files/downloads/6961EN_coloredimages.pdf`

# Errata

Although we have taken every care to ensure the accuracy of our content, mistakes do happen. If you find a mistake in one of our books—maybe a mistake in the text or the code—we would be grateful if you would report this to us. By doing so, you can save other readers from frustration and help us improve subsequent versions of this book. If you find any errata, please report them by visiting `http://www.packtpub.com/submit-errata`, selecting your book, clicking on the **errata submission form** link, and entering the details of your errata. Once your errata are verified, your submission will be accepted and the errata will be uploaded on our website, or added to any list of existing errata, under the Errata section of that title. Any existing errata can be viewed by selecting your title from `http://www.packtpub.com/support`.

# Piracy

Piracy of copyright material on the Internet is an ongoing problem across all media. At Packt, we take the protection of our copyright and licenses very seriously. If you come across any illegal copies of our works, in any form, on the Internet, please provide us with the location address or website name immediately so that we can pursue a remedy.

Please contact us at `copyright@packtpub.com` with a link to the suspected pirated material.

We appreciate your help in protecting our authors, and our ability to bring you valuable content.

# Questions

You can contact us at `questions@packtpub.com` if you are having a problem with any aspect of the book, and we will do our best to address it.

# 1
# Introduction to vCenter Operations Manager

In this chapter, we'll cover:

- What is vCenter Operations Manager?
- Benefits of troubleshooting with vC Ops
- Benefits of capacity planning with vC Ops
- Feature comparison of different versions
- What is vCenter Operations Manager Suite?
- Licensing versions
- Using vC Ops with other solutions

## What is vCenter Operations Manager?

**vCenter Operations Manager**, also known as **vC Ops**, is a VMware product that allows IT administrators to monitor their virtual environments in the most efficient way. It also aids in design and capacity planning. vC Ops allows us administrators and IT managers to have visibility into our entire virtual infrastructure and goes beyond the simple alarms and performance charts offered in vCenter Server alone. It offers dashboards, alerts, and several detailed reports to help us better assess our environments. We can even monitor several different vCenter environments by simply configuring vC Ops to connect with any vCenter Server that we have in our environment. vC Ops is a vApp consisting of two virtual appliances that can be downloaded from the VMware website. It comes with a management plugin that's easily installed on the vSphere client. Alternatively we can browse the management site directly, if preferable. With vSphere Version 5.1 and above, we can also use vSphere Web Client to manage vC Ops and we can find embedded metrics within the summary pages for most of the objects in our virtual infrastructure.

As we can see from the following screenshot, the default dashboard offered in all the licensed versions of vC Ops above the Foundation edition holds a lot of information. We get an idea of the three major metrics, or badges, that vC Ops tells us about: Health, Risk, and Efficiency. Dashboards such as the one shown in the following screenshot can quickly give us an insight into the things that are happening in our environment and visually point out any errors or issues inside our environment that may have cause for more investigation.

Although vCenter Server comes with its own alarms and performance charts, vC Ops actually *learns* about our environment and reports alerts based on that. In fact, it's recommended that we let vC Ops run for a month after the initial installation before we start looking at the metrics and going through the reports. vCenter Server has several alarms that will show up on our vSphere Client, but we need to set these alarms with hard triggers. For example, in the following screenshot, we can see the vCenter 5.1 alarm triggers for **Host memory usage** in vSphere Web Client. It shows that if the memory usage for a physical host is above 90 percent for five minutes or longer, it will give us a warning. If the host memory usage is above 95 percent for five minutes or longer, it will give us a critical error.

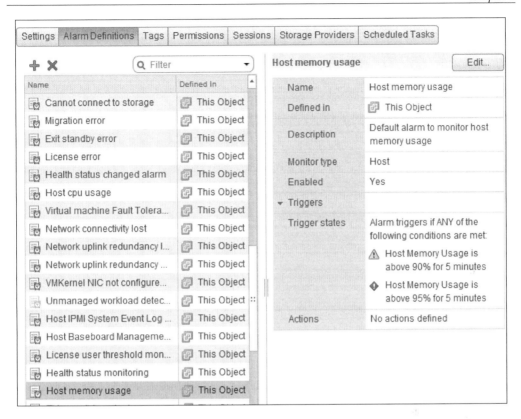

For an alarm like this, a rigid or static trigger threshold may be appropriate. Memory should really not be at more than 95 percent utilization for too long. In that situation, we would want to add more memory to that host or perhaps vMotion VMs to another host if we have that option. However, what if we have an alarm triggered for CPU usage of a virtual machine? If this virtual machine consistently runs with high CPU usage because it's supposed to, vCenter will still tell us there is a critical error. Since vC Ops actually learns our environment, it will tell us that this is not an anomalous behavior, and we may not need to worry about it. Another example of when this is useful would be if a VM routinely runs scheduled tasks that cause CPU or memory utilization to be high for a brief time during the day. vCenter alarms would trigger everyday or every time this happens. vC Ops will learn this behavior, thereby reducing the barrage of alerts admins receive everyday. vC Ops will still tell us that CPU usage runs high via badge scores, such as Workload or Stress, so we don't have to worry about missing information either.

Other than immediate notifications and alarms found throughout the dashboards and reports, vC Ops also gives us visibility into longer-term issues and helps us know whether it's safe to add or remove VMs as well as physical resources to our environment.

# Benefits of troubleshooting with vC Ops

As mentioned in the previous section, vC Ops actually understands our environment and reports anomalous behavior. This is not to say that if a VM is always using 100 percent of its storage, vC Ops will let you know that. It will also let you know how long it's been happening and the normal range for the VM. If we zoom in on the **Workload** badge, as shown in the following screenshot, we can see that it shows CPU usage, memory usage, disk I/O, and network I/O. The blue bar above each graph shows the normal range for each metric. If it were outside of that normal range, that would indicate anomalous behavior. This can be very helpful for troubleshooting because now we can dive in and see what's changed. From vCenter Server alone, we can see some historical data, and we can see real-time metrics, but without doing some pretty intense math, we won't know the normal range.

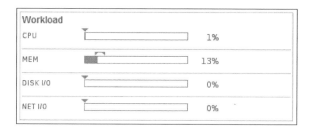

Another benefit you get with vC Ops, which you wouldn't necessarily see in the vCenter Server performance data, is that you can check whether VMs are undersized. An undersized VM is a virtual machine with less compute resources than it actually needs to perform properly. Again, this is not based solely on random peaks or bursts, but rather on historical and present data that has been run through algorithms, and vC Ops lets us know how much compute the VM should be assigned for it to work efficiently. So, for instance, if an application is running slow, or even slow at particular times in a day consistently, we would be able to open vC Ops, highlight the affected machine, and then go to the **Planning** tab. From here, we can see how much time this VM has been running without enough memory or CPU, for example, and it will also tell us how much additional resources it recommends.

One of the most interesting benefits is when you pair vC Ops with vCenter Configuration Manager. Again, let's say we have an application that's all of a sudden running slow or sporadically. If we open vC Ops and highlight the problematic VM again, we can find the recent events and tasks that have been performed on that VM. On this page, we can also see a graph with the performance of the VM. We can see where the performance spiked and also the events that correlated with that timeframe. Perhaps the event would be something similar to "VM RAM was changed from 10 GB to 2 GB". Even before we use vCenter Configuration Manager, we've narrowed down the issue to being lack of memory. Now, if we check with vCenter Configuration Manager, we may be able to see which administrator made that change, if that change was made from  vCenter Configuration Manager.

The last benefit I'm going to bring up here, though there are certainly more, is the easy way to find relationships between VMs and other vSphere inventory objects. So, why is finding the relationship between a VM and what it's connected to important? Let's look at our previous two scenarios, where we had an application running slow on a VM. If we were to look at the VM, it could show that things are running slow, but we may be unable to find the reason immediately. However, if we look at the relationships between them, there may be a common denominator, such as a datastore or host, that is actually causing the issue. We may see that all the VMs on that particular datastore or host are running poorly, but if we correct the error at the root of the problem, we'll correct the issues on all the VMs connected to it. Using vCenter alone, we might have taken a lot longer to figure out this correlation, but because we can see all the relationships mapped out for us, it's easier to do a root cause analysis. See the following two screenshots for illustrations of how this might look. The following example is of the **Overview** section of the **Environment** tab. It shows all of the elements across the environment from the top down but highlights those related to, for example, a selected VM.

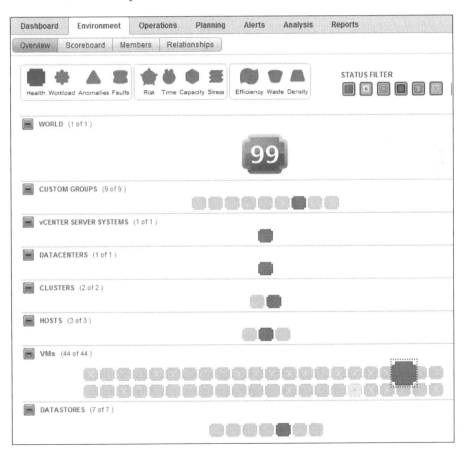

The following example, found under the **Relationships** section of the **Environment** tab, gives you a different view. It shows only the components that are in a direct relationship with the component you have selected in the left-hand side pane.

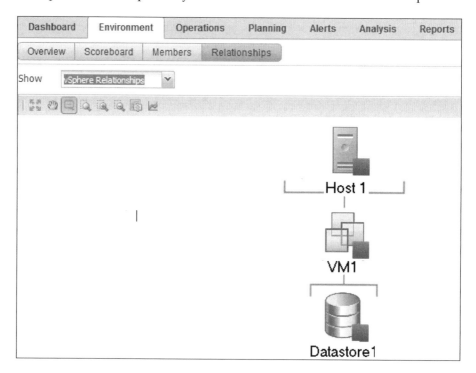

# Benefits of capacity planning with vC Ops

VMware used to have a solution called vCenter Capacity IQ. In early 2012, VMware stopped selling Capacity IQ and put all of the capacity planning features from Capacity IQ into vC Ops. We can upgrade vCenter Capacity IQ licenses to vC Ops licenses. vCenter itself doesn't really offer much by way of capacity planning. Obviously, we can look at how much space we have free on our datastores as well as how many compute resources we have free, but it would still be an estimate. With vC Ops, we take the guesswork out of it with the use of oversized VM reporting and what-if scenarios.

The great thing about vC Ops is that it actually has a lot of capacity management features in every view and dashboard. No matter where we've drilled in, we'll be able to see information about how much storage or compute resources are left. However, most of the capacity planning features can be easily found under the **Planning** and **Analysis** tabs. Here, we can find information, not only on how much storage or compute a VM is using, but also what the trends have been for future planning purposes. For instance, you might be able to see that a datastore has been losing about 2 GB of free space every week. If the datastore is 1 TB, vC Ops can estimate when we might run out of space.

Much like the undersized VM analysis discussed in the troubleshooting section, we also have data on which VMs are oversized. Many times applications and/or application owners will ask for outrageous amounts of CPU or memory. There are also cases where we perform physical to virtual migrations to convert a physical server to a virtual server and we just leave the original amount of compute resources even if it's not necessary. vCenter Server is never going to tell us that we've over allocated memory or CPU, for example, to a VM. vC Ops, however, will show us a full report on the VMs on which we can reclaim compute resources and how much can be reclaimed. This may seem like a small reclamation of resources, but let's say we have 100 VMs, and 25 of them are using an extra two vCPUs, then we can essentially reclaim 50 vCPUs as well as reduce CPU contention within our environment.

Probably the most interesting benefit of using vC Ops to do our capacity planning is the what-if scenarios. We can actually click on a link under the **Planning** tab to pull up a what-if scenario wizard. For example, with this wizard, we can manually input the number of VMs we want to add, and it will output how that will affect the current environment. We can also have it automatically input the variables using trending analytics for our environment. vC Ops will take a look at the average size of our VMs, analyze any pertinent historical data, and then tell us if we have enough resources to add a certain amount of VMs. This is an incredibly powerful tool that most normal admins would not be able to replicate through the use of a simple script with simple mathematics.

# Feature comparison of versions

A number of versions of vC Ops are available. The following is a quick overview of the various versions.

# What is vCenter Operations Manager Suite?

The main focus of this book is vC Ops although we do get into some of the other components of the suite. VMware has historically sold the current components of the suite separately. Recently though, they've decided it would be beneficial to bundle them in a suite. The components of the suite are as follows:

- vCenter Operations Manager
- vCenter Configuration Manager
- vFabric Hyperic
- vCenter Infrastructure Navigator
- vCenter Chargeback Manager

For more information on these components, check the documentation given on VMware.com.

# Licensing versions

Not every component comes in the vC Ops suite. It depends on which version of the license has been purchased. The versions of the suite are as follows:

- Foundation
- Standard
- Advanced
- Enterprise

The versions of the vC Ops suite should not be confused with the versions of the vCloud suite. They are separate items.

 It should be noted that VMware did announce during VMworld 2013 that vCenter Operations Manager Suite will be included in all vCloud Suite 5.5 editions. At the time of writing this book, vCloud Suite 5.5 and vSphere have not been released.

| Edition | Foundation | Standard | Advanced | Enterprise |
|---|---|---|---|---|
| Description | vSphere Performance and Health | vSphere Monitoring, Performance and Capacity Optimization | Virtual and Physical Infrastructure Operations, including Monitoring, Performance, Capacity and Configuration Management | Hybrid Cloud Infrastructure Operation, including OS- and Application-Level Monitoring, Performance, Capacity and Configuration Management |
| vCenter Operations Management Suite Components | | | | |
| vCenter Operations Manager* | ∘ | ∘ | ∘ | ∘ |
| vCenter Configuration Manager* | | | ∘ | ∘ |
| vFabric Hyperic* | | | ∘ | ∘ |
| vCenter Infrastructure Navigator | | | ∘ | ∘ |
| vCenter Chargeback Manager | | | ∘ | ∘ |

As of Version 5.7, vC Ops licensing works in the following way. This chart was taken directly from the VMware.com website.

By looking at the chart, **Foundation** and **Standard** look the same, as do Advanced and Enterprise. However, that's not actually the case. Currently the Foundation license is included in every version of vCenter. It does not give us insights using historical data, it only reports in real time. However, it will store the historical data if we decide to upgrade the license at a later date. Foundation doesn't really offer much by way of capacity planning either. It's really more of just an extension of our current alerts that we get from vCenter.

As shown in the chart, Standard gives us all that is included in Foundation, as well as the capacity features. It is basically a full version of vCenter Operations Manager. The Advanced and Enterprise versions give us what is really more of a suite with the components mentioned earlier. The difference between these being that Enterprise gives us more OS- and application-level monitoring and Advanced really just gives us the VM-level monitoring.

# Using vC Ops with other solutions

There are several plugins or adapters to vC Ops that will extend our monitoring capabilities even further. One plugin that came out in the last year or so is vCenter Operations Manager for Horizon View. Through the use of vC Ops adapters, we can now monitor our Horizon View virtual desktop implementations. This gives us custom dashboards that give us a lot more insight than we've had before. If you've ever run a VDI environment, you must be well aware that the ability to pinpoint our problem areas quickly is a necessity. Other VMware solutions it will connect to are vCloud Director 1.5.0 and above.

There are several storage adapters for vC Ops as well. Among these are the EMC Smarts Adapter, EMC Symmetrix Adapter, EMC VNX Adapter, and NetApp Adapter. There are also several monitoring solutions that vC Ops can connect with to get a view of your whole environment, such as HP BAC Adapter, HP SiteScope Adapter, IBM Tivoli Monitoring Adapter, and Microsoft SCOM Adapter. It will also plug into Oracle Enterprise Manager to help you monitor your Oracle databases.

In most cases, after connecting vC Ops to these adapters, we need to browse to a custom site other than our vC Ops management site. These sites will have custom dashboards set up with information from the product(s) we are connected to. At present, this information does not really affect the regular vC Ops dashboards. You will still see the same information there that you would see if you did not have the adapters installed and collecting data.

# Summary

In this chapter, we discussed what vCenter Operations Manager is. It's a solution that allows us to monitor our virtual infrastructure as well as plan for future capacity issues that may arise. We then discussed some of the benefits of troubleshooting our virtual environments as well as doing some capacity planning with the help of vCenter Operations Manager. It's also important to keep in mind that there are several different versions of vC Ops, and it is possible to get it in a bundle with vCenter Configuration Manager, vFabric Hyperic, vCenter Infrastructure Navigator, and vCenter Chargeback Manager. Finally, we went over some of the other hardware and software solutions that we can integrate into our vCenter Operations Manager and/or suite, such as storage arrays and other third-party monitoring solutions.

In the next chapter, we'll actually get started with installing vCenter Operations Manager. Along with this, we'll discuss how to prepare your environment and vCenter Server specifically. We'll also cover some practical information about changing or adding licenses, as that can be a bit of a hassle with the current version of vC Ops. We'll end by configuring some basic setup items to get vC Ops running and usable.

# 2
# Installing vCenter Operations Manager

The vC Ops manager can be installed in a few different ways. In this chapter, we'll go with the most common way, that is, by using the vApp provided by VMware. It is also possible to download and install the product on a Windows or Linux server. The vApp comes preconfigured with the resources we need and does not require the use of another Windows or Linux license as well. In this chapter, we will cover the basic installation procedures and considerations such as the ones in the following list:

- System requirements
- Preparing the vCenter Server
- Deploying the vCenter Operations Manager's vApp
- Configuring the vCenter Operations Manager
- vC Ops' custom dashboard
- Upgrading vC Ops

# System requirements

The requirements mentioned in this section are all for vCenter Operations Manager 5.7.1. These requirements are subject to change in future releases of vC Ops. The software requirements are as follows:

- ESX/ESXi Version 4.0 and above
- vCenter Server 4.0 Update 2 and above
- If using the vCenter Infrastructure Navigator, it must be at least Version 2.0
- The software should work on the following browsers:
    - Apple Safari 6
    - Google Chrome 24 and 25
    - Internet Explorer 8.0 and 9.0
    - Mozilla Firefox 18 and higher
- The hardware requirements depending on the size of our virtual environments are as follows:
    - 4 to 16 vCPUs
    - 16 to 34 GB of memory
    - Add disk space as needed via extra hard drives

 For more information on adding disk space to the UI VM or Analytics VM within the vC Ops vApp please, see the *VMware KB* article 2016022 at `http://kb.vmware.com/selfservice/microsites/search.do?language=en_US&cmd=displayKC&externalId=2016022`.

# Preparing the vCenter Server

It's assumed that we have vCenter running at this point, and it has been configured with proper networking and storage to access it via our network and access VMs residing on the physical hosts. To begin with, we need to make sure the ports are open between vCenter and vC Ops. If there aren't firewalls in between, then you can skip this part. The ports to open are as follows:

- 22: SSH for command-line management
- 80: HTTP which is redirected to HTTPS

- 443: HTTPS for GUI management
- 1194: Tunnel between UI VM and Analytics VM

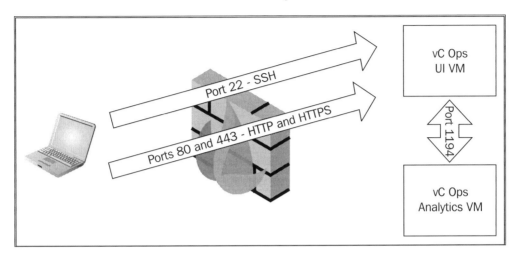

As you may know, vC Ops comes as vApp that consists of two virtual machines: the **(UI) User Interface** VM and the Analytics VM. The UI VM is what allows us to access the information, and the Analytics VM is the data collector that contains a Postgres database to store all the information. Because vC Ops comes as vApp, we can do some interesting things with IP addresses on vCenter to automatically assign IPs to our virtual machines within the vApp. We do this using IP pools, which are called **network protocol profiles** in newer versions of vSphere. We do not need IP pools to automatically assign IPs to vApp VMs. We are able to statically assign IPs to each VM during the setup. However, IP pools are necessary to power on the vC Ops vApp.

vC Ops can be installed as a standalone solution instead of vApp. In that case, you would download **vCenter Operations Manager Standalone**. The two VMs would just be individual VMs with no ties to vApp. You would want to do this in an environment with only one physical host or in a cluster without DRS enabled. If you choose to enable it this way, you must power off the UI VM 10 minutes before the Analytics VM. Then to power on, you must power on the Analytics VM 10 minutes before the UI VM according to VMware KB 2013695. For more information, refer to http://kb.vmware.com/selfservice/microsites/search. do?language=en_US&cmd=displayKC&externalId=2013695.

The following steps will help you in configuring an IP pool:

1. Open your vSphere Web Client and log in to the client.

2. Click on **Networking**.

3. Select the vSwitch you'd like to configure it on. If you have multiple vSwitches, you most likely to put it where your management or production VMs reside.

4. Select the **Manage** tab.

5. Select **Network Protocol Profile** as shown in the following screenshot:

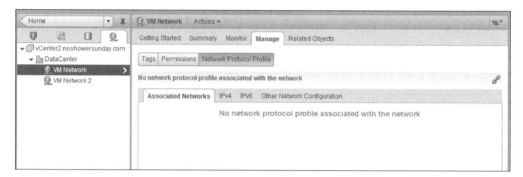

6. Click on the link icon to associate a network protocol profile, and select the network you'd like to associate it with. Click on **Next**.

7. Give it a name, for example, Network Protocol Profile – vC Ops. Click on **Next**.

8. Configure the networking as shown in the following screenshot. Remember we need to use network settings that are appropriate for our network. Since we're going to assign static IPs to virtual machines, there's no need to use the network protocol profile to hand out IP addresses. Be sure to leave the **Enable IP Pool** option unchecked. This will allow us to configure fixed IPs on the VMs themselves in case something goes wrong with vApp. Configuring an IP pool is still a necessary step though, because vApp can get other network information such as DNS and default gateway IP addresses.

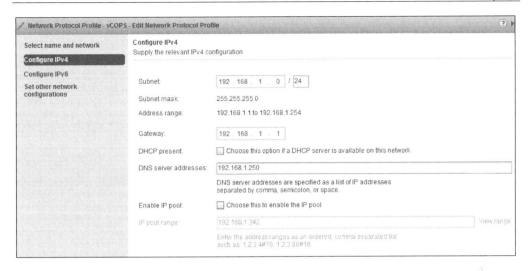

9. Configure IPv6 if necessary.

10. Add the name of your domain in the **Set other network configuration** portion of the wizard.

11. Click on **Finish** unless you need to configure advanced settings such as proxy information.

This is all we have to do to get vCenter ready before the deployment of our vApp. IP pools can be somewhat confusing, and while it's not in the scope of this book to define them, it would be beneficial to understand how they work. VMware's website, as well as several independent blogs, contain all the information we would ever want to know about IP pools.

Refer to the following URLs for information about IP pools:

*   http://wahlnetwork.com/2012/12/11/understanding-and-configuring-vsphere-ip-pools/
*   http://www.yellow-bricks.com/2012/02/02/creating-an-ip-pool-for-vc-ops/

Please note we'll be using the vSphere Web Client in this book. Although, it is still possible to use the traditional vSphere Client as of vSphere 5.5, the web client is the future, so it's good to get used to it.

# Deploying the vCenter Operations Manager's vApp

Now we can move on to deploying the vC Ops app. To deploy the vC Ops vApp, the steps are as follows:

1. Open your vSphere Web Client and log in to it.

2. Go back to the **Home** page and then click on the **Hosts and Clusters** inventory view.

3. Right-click on the host where you'd like to place the vApp and select **Deploy OVF Template**.

4. From the **Select Source** page, click on the local file and browse to the location from where you downloaded vC Ops. You may need to change the file type to .ova to find it. Click on **Next**.

5. Click on **Next** through the next few pages of the wizard to accept the **EULA** (**end-user license agreement**).

6. Choose the name for your vApp and where to place it. Then, click on **Next**.

7. Under the **Select Configuration** page, select the proper configuration (see the following information box) for your environment and click on **Next**.

The three configuration options are as follows:

**Small**: This configuration is used when the number of VMs is less than 1500 and requires 4 vCPUs and 16 GB of memory for the vApp

**Medium**: This is used when the number of VMs is between 1500 to 3000 and requires 8 vCPUs and 25 GB of memory for the vApp

**Large**: This configuration is used when the number of VMs is more than 3000 and requires 16 vCPUs and 34 GB of memory for the vApp

How we choose between these three options really depends. If we don't have many computer resources, and it's just not possible for us to give up 16 vCPUs and 34 GB of memory, then we should probably pick the small or medium configuration. Remember that 16 vCPUs, even though it's split between two VMs within the vApp, is going to cause some CPU contention. We want to make sure we have the necessary hardware to allow for whichever option we choose. Also, if we're concerned about growing larger in the future but don't have the necessary resources now, we can always increase the amount of memory and vCPU later on.

8. On the **Select Storage** page, select the data store where you would like to place the vApp as well as whether you would like to make it thin or thick provisioned. If you're using this in a production environment, it's recommended to make it thick provisioned.

9. On the **Setup Networks** list, select the network you'd like to put the VMs on. We'll also make the IP allocation **Static – Manual** so the VMs always have the same IP address. Click on **Next**.

10. Set the time zone in which you're located in the **Customize Template** page.

11. Then expand the **Networking Properties** on this page and input the IP addresses you'd like to allocate to each VM as shown in the following screenshot. Click on **Next**.

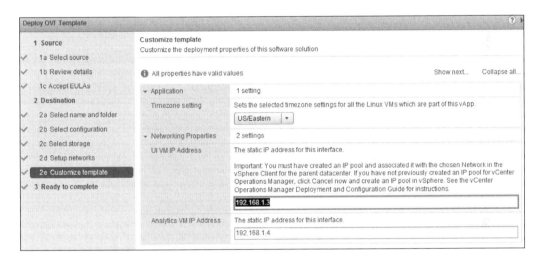

12. Click on **Finish** to exit the wizard and start the deployment.

The deployment might take several minutes to complete. We can see the status in the **Recent Tasks** window at the top-right corner of our vSphere Web Client. When that is done, we can click on the vC Ops vApp and click on **Power on vApp**. It may also take several minutes to power on. Keep in mind that it will start the Analytics VM first and then start the UI VM. After they've completed the initial startup, which will take several minutes, the consoles will look something similar to this:

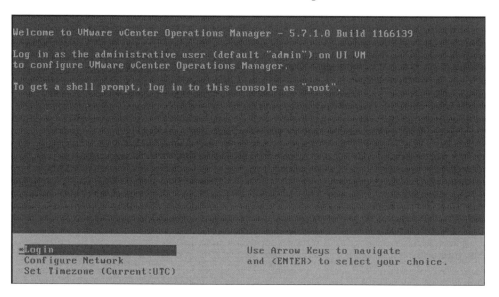

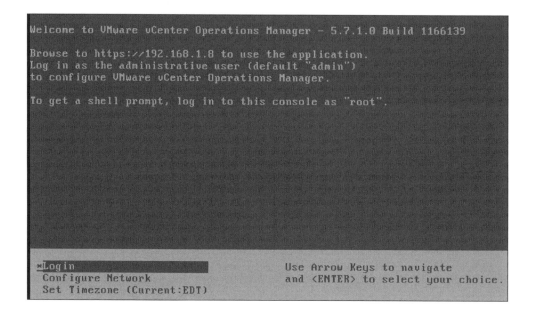

# Configuring the vCenter Operations Manager

The following section explains the process of configuring vCenter Operations Manager. Let's look into the Initial Setup Wizard.

We can now perform the initial setup of vC Ops by browsing to the IP address of the UI VM. We are presented with the **Initial Setup Wizard** where we can assign credentials and authenticate it to vCenter. The first screen is where we fill in the **Virtual Appliance Details**. This will have our vCenter information as shown in the following screenshot:

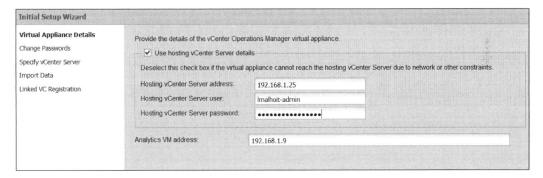

On the **Change Passwords** screen, we'll configure passwords for both the admin and the root account. The admin account is to access the UI, and the root account is for logging into the console in the event we need shell access to perform CLI operations. In the vCenter server, the **Specify vCenter Server** screen allows us to specify that we will be monitoring with vC Ops. We also have the option of specifying not only the registration user but a collection user as well. If we choose to use different credentials for the collection user, we must ensure this user has at least read access to the objects within the vSphere client.

If this is your first installation, the **Import Data** screen will probably not be important. If you had historical data from some vCenter extension, you could import it here. If this is not the first installation, we would also be able to import information from previous installtions of vC Ops here. Also, the next screen, **Linked VC Registration**, may or may not apply to your environment. If you're connecting your vCenter servers from different sites using **Linked Mode**, then you can supply that information here. Keep in mind that if a firewall exists between the vCenter servers, vC Ops will need to have access to both the sites. When we click on **Finish** at the end of the wizard, we will see a window with a status bar that tells us vC Ops is registering with vCenter. When that's done, we'll see a screen similar to the one that follows:

Take note that at the top-right corner, under where it says **vCenter Operations Manager Administration**, it reads **Version 5.7.1**; however, under licensing information, it still reads **5.6**. That's normal! They use the same licenses, so don't be alarmed if you see this. Also notice that it says the **License Mode** is **Foundation** due to the fact that we have yet to assign a proper license to our vC Ops instance.

The horizontal tab navigation allows us to configure many different aspects of our vC Ops appliance. Let's start with the **Registration** page. The **Registration Status** is purely informational, but if we move down to the **vCenter Server Metrics Profile**, you'll see there is a drop-down menu that lets you choose either **Balanced Profile** or **Full Profile**. This is a new feature of vC Ops 5.7. If you are monitoring several objects, you may want to choose **Balanced Profile** because it offers a reduced set of metrics allowing you to monitor even more. On this page, you can also add new vCenter servers and register vC Ops with vCenter Configuration Manager Registration.

On the **SMTP/SNMP** page, we can enable and enter our mail server settings if we wish to receive alerts from vC Ops via e-mail. We can also enable and enter the information for SNMP to allow vC Ops to send alerts via SNMP traps to third-party monitoring solutions such as **NAGIOS** or **Zenoss**.

The **SSL** tab is pretty self-explanatory. If we want to use a certificate from a certificate authority, such as **Thawt** or **Verisign**, we can import the `.pem` file here. Otherwise, we will just be using the self-signed certificate that gets created automatically during the installation. Using a self-signed certificate will work, but it's not secure. Most self-signed certificates have unreasonably long expiry dates, making it is much easier to perform a man-in-the-middle attack.

For more information on man-in-the-middle attacks, please see this article:

`http://en.wikipedia.org/wiki/Man-in-the-middle_attack`

For more information on configuring a CA certificate for vC Ops, please refer to VMware KB 2046591:

`http://kb.vmware.com/selfservice/microsites/search.do?language=en_US&cmd=displayKC&externalId=2046591`

On the **Status** tab, we have a lot of useful tools and information for troubleshooting our vC Ops environment. We can start and stop the vC Ops service as well as see the status information on the service. We can also download diagnostic information in the event in which we need to further investigate issues with our vC Ops product.

The **Update** tab allows us to browse to an updated vC Ops file and import it. Then just click on the **Update** button, and it should update everything for you. Then, we have the **Account** tab, which is where you can change passwords for your admin and root accounts.

# Assigning licenses

As you may recall, we are still working with the Foundation license mode that does not give us any of the historical data and capacity information we need. In this section, we'll go through assigning proper licensing for vC Ops using the vSphere Web Client.

The steps for assigning the license are as follows:

1. Open the web client and go to the **Administration** page.

2. Then click on **Licenses** under **Licensing** and click on the **Solutions** tab. We should see our vCenter Operations Manager on this page now that we have it registered as shown in the following screenshot:

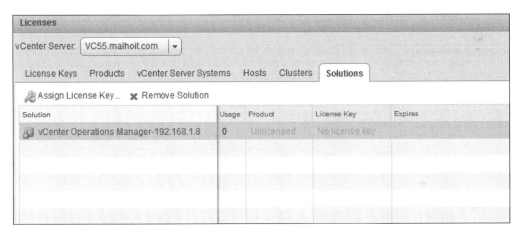

3. Click on the **Assign License Key** button. We can click on the drop-down menu on this pop-up page to select **Assign a new license key**.

4. Enter your license key and any description you'd like to give it here.

5. After you click on **OK**, it will populate other fields with proper information from your key.

That's pretty easy. What happens if we need to change the license because we upgraded to the next version though? We can click on **Assign License Key** again and give it a new key. Don't expect it to be updated right away though. This is updated every 20 minutes or so. You can either go grab some coffee or perform the following manual update procedure:

1. Open the console on your UI VM and log in with the root username.

2. Type the following command to switch to the admin user:

   ```
   su - admin
   ```

3. Run the following command to update your license:

   ```
   vC Ops-admin license update
   ```

4. You can see if it's updated by looking at the SKU, using this command:

   ```
   vC Ops-admin license sku
   ```

5. Then type exit and restart the service using the following command:

   ```
   service vC Opsadmin restart
   ```

For more information on updating vC Ops licenses manually, you can check out the VMware KB article KB2042698 – vCenter Operations Manager 5.x license status fails to update after the license is applied:

```
http://kb.vmware.com/selfservice/microsites/search.
do?language=en_US&cmd=displayKC&externalId=2042698
```

Really, at this point, we have a basic usable vCenter Operations Manager solution. It will automatically start collecting data for all of the resources in your vCenter environment. Again, keep in mind that vC Ops will learn about our environment, so we need to give it at least a couple of weeks, if not a month, to collect and analyze the data before we start going through it.

We can make a few configuration changes while in the regular vC Ops UI. If you click on the **Configuration** link at the top-right side of vC Ops, you'll be presented with a configuration pop up. This will let you manage policies, group types, and display settings.

# Managing policies

When you select the **Manage Policies** tab, the default policy will already be populated. You can click on that default policy to modify it or create a new policy. In here, we can change thresholds if the default settings aren't what you're looking for. We can also change capacity settings along with what we're monitoring. We can set up some basic alert configurations in which we can specify whether we'd like to be (or not be) alerted about certain things. Then, we can change the forecast and trends options.

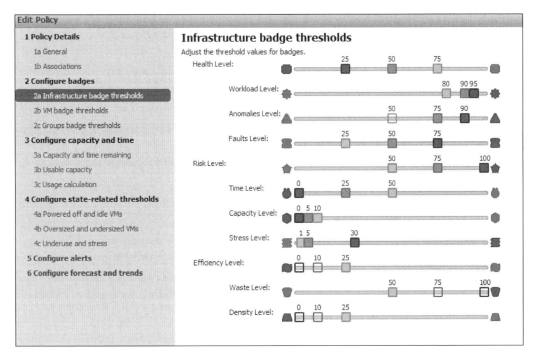

# Managing group types

We can add, delete, and modify group types as well. A group type is any collection of objects with a common configuration or feature. For instance, the **Location** group type would be a collection of objects at the same site. The default group types are shown in the following screenshot. We can only modify and delete group types that are managed by the user though.

**Manage Group Types**

Create, edit and delete user-created group types.

| Name | Managed By |
| --- | --- |
| vCM Machine Groups | Adapter |
| World | Adapter |
| Folder | Adapter |
| Application | Adapter |
| Environment | User |
| Function | User |
| Service Level Objective | User |
| Location | User |
| Department | User |
| Security Zone | User |

# Managing display settings

This is probably the configuration option we will actually use the most. In here, we can change the views to show whatever times we like (for example, daily). What I find I do most is to change **Report Views**. Under the **Reports** heading, we can specify **Report Period**, which by default is **Monthly**. However, if we want to generate reports of metrics from the last day or week, it's as simple as changing the dropdown as shown in the following screenshot:

For more information on deploying and configuring vCenter Operations Manager, please refer to the *vApp Deployment and Configuration Guide – vCenter Operations Manager 5.7* documentation found on the VMware website.

# vC Ops custom dashboard

The vC Ops custom dashboard is the part of vC Ops that a lot of users either miss or think that it is only necessary when you use add-ins. However, this can be utilized to create custom dashboards, alerts, add user permissions, create groups, create super metrics (user-defined combinations of metrics), and all sorts of other good stuff.

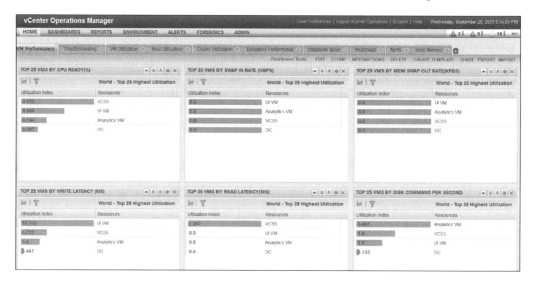

On the home screen, we have several tabs with groups that are automatically populated. Under the **VM Performance** tab, we get lists of the top VM resource hogs as shown in the previous screenshot. Under the **Troubleshooting** tab, we can see the symptoms of VMs by their relationships as well as Interesting Metrics. We can also see **VM**, **Host and Cluster Utilization**, **Datastore Performance**, **Datastore Space**, **Heatmaps**, **Alerts**, and **Host Memory**. A lot of this information will also be visible via the regular dashboard that we saw earlier.

 Custom dashboards are only available with the Enterprise version of vC Ops.

# Configuring user permissions

We have an option to add administrators, operators, and users by default while still in the custom dashboard. To add users, perform the following steps:

1. Hover over the **Admin** tab in the custom dashboard.

2. Click on **Security**.

3. Select a group from the left-hand side of the pane; in this case, we'll choose **Administrators**.

4. In the **User Accounts** pane, we'll either click on the icon to add a user which will allow us to create a local user as an admin, or we can click on the icon to import a user from LDAP. If you're adding the user from LDAP, you will need to add an LDAP (or Active Directory) host and configure it with the parameters appropriate for your environment. Then you'll sync it and select a user that is populated in that group.

5. Once we press **OK**, our user will be added as follows:

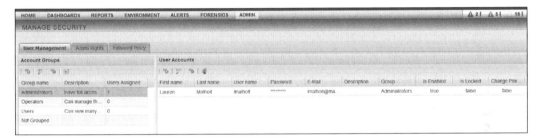

# Adapters

Adapters are hooks that we can use to display resources within vC Ops. We can use adapters to connect to other things in VMware as well as third-party solutions. You won't need to worry about this for a basic setup of vC Ops though. Most of the VMware adapters are in there by default such as the **Infrastructure Navigator** adapter, **vCenter** adapter, and so on as (shown in the next screenshot). Here, we can edit these adapters or delete them as well. To manage adapters, follow the given steps:

1. Hover over the **Environment** tab and then hover over **Configuration**.

2. In the **Configuration** menu, click on **Adapter Instances**.

3. Highlight the adapter you would like to modify or delete:

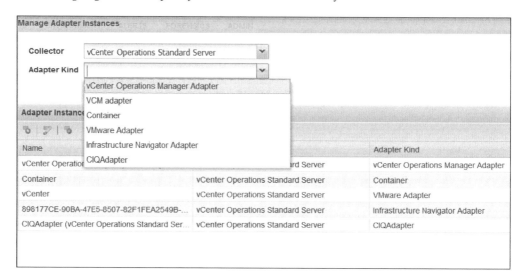

# Resources

Resources are essentially objects that we're monitoring with vC Ops. Most of our resources will be discovered and populated automatically upon the initial setup. However, in the case that resources have embedded adapters or no adapters, we will need to manually discover or set them up.

To add resources, follow these steps:

1. Hover over the **Environment** tab and click on **Environment Overview**.
2. Click on the **List** tab.
3. Click on the **Discover Resources** icon as shown in the following screenshot:

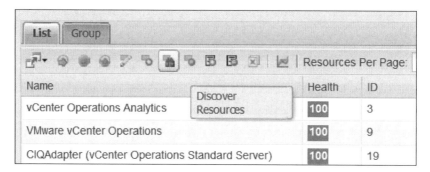

4. From the drop-down menu, select a **Collector**, **Adapter Kind**, **Adapter Instance**, **Discovery Info**, and **Resource Kind**:

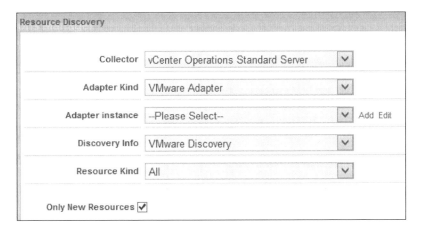

5. Then click on **OK** to start the discovery.

6. If there are any resources available, you can add them here.

7. If you need to manually add a resource, just click the icon to the left of **Discover Resources** called **Add Resource**.

We can assign resource tags to our resources that will then allow us to group resources in our custom dashboard by the tag it's been given. Resource tags are user-defined labels that we assign. Resources can also be grouped by location using Google Maps keys if you have different physical sites you're monitoring. In that case, we would assign Google Maps keys to our resources and it would automatically know where these resources are physically located.

There are several configuration possibilities and very advanced options we can set up using custom dashboards. For a full list along with how-to's, please see the *VMware vCenter Operations Manager Administration Guide – Custom User Interface* documentation found on the VMware site.

# Upgrading vC Ops

Upgrading vC Ops is a fairly simple procedure due to its vApp architecture. When a new version of vC Ops comes out, we simply need to download the `.pak` file that comes from VMware and apply that to our vApp.

To upgrade vC Ops, complete the following steps:

1.  Log in to your admin portal by browsing to `https://<IP_Address>/admin` and providing the admin credentials.
2.  Click on the **Update** tab.
3.  Click on **Browse** to find the `.pak` file you've downloaded from `VMware.com`.
4.  Follow the wizard to complete the upgrade.
5.  Upgrade your license if necessary. For some of the minor releases, this is not necessary. You will need to check the VMware documentation for information on this.

Keep in mind you'll need to wait for about 20 minutes for the license to upgrade. Until that has completed, or you've manually upgraded the licenses using the steps mentioned earlier in this chapter, some of the features of the new version may not be available.

# Summary

In this chapter, we went over some of the prerequisites for setting up vCenter Operations Manager as well as preparing vCenter before the actual deployment of the vC Ops vApp. We needed to set up IP pools in order to make all the networking on our vApp work properly. We then deployed the vApp and went through the basic configuration to get a working vC Ops solution.

After going through the initial configuration, we went through some of the highlights of the vC Ops custom dashboard, which is only found in the Enterprise version. We can customize many options in vC Ops using the Enterprise version that allows administrators to easily monitor high priority hardware and applications.

In the next chapter, we will go over Dashboards and Badges, which are tools that give you a quick visual as to what your environment looks like and any problems you might be seeing. We'll see how to navigate vC Ops quickly and efficiently so that we're better able to understand our environment and what's going on within it.

# 3

# Dashboards and Badges

When talking with people, I've found that one of the reasons they get frustrated while using vCenter Operations Manager is they're not sure how to navigate it and don't understand what all the dashboard objects mean. This chapter will focus on defining all that and will give practical examples of how we might use it in our environment.

We'll cover the following topics in this chapter:

- Navigation overview
- Major badges
- Minor badges
- Heat maps

# Navigation overview

The vC Ops UI, which we can get to either by browsing to `https://<IP_Address_of_UI_VM` or via the plugin in vCenter, by default looks as shown in the following screenshot:

 To enable a plugin within the vSphere client, we must click on **Plug-ins** and then on **Manage Plug-ins**. Then, click on the link that says Download and install. Once the plug-in is installed, we can click on the Home page within the vSphere client to get to the solution.

As we can see on the left, there is a standard tree structure with **World** at the very top while in the Hosts and Clusters view. World just refers to our entire environment. It is then broken down from vCenter to all the containers underneath it as we would actually see via the vCenter client. While still in the left pane, we can click on the group's icon to show various groups we set up to connect our objects. We can create new groups by clicking on **Actions** in the center pane and then selecting **Create New Group**. Then finally, we have the Datastore view that also shows us a tree with **World** at the top. Then, the group is broken down and eventually, all of our datastores including local datastores are broken down by vCenter.

On the right-hand side, we see a summary of alerts: **Critical**, **Immediate**, **Warning**, and **Info**. It will show the alerts specific to the object we have selected from the tree on the left-hand side. It also shows a summary of the **Health**, **Risk**, and **Efficiency** (major badges) scores as well as the minor badge scores for the object selected from the tree. We can minimize both the left pane (tree structure) and the right pane (alerts) by clicking on the double arrow at the top left and right, respectively.

# The Dashboard tab

At the center of the UI, we have the main pane with several tabs: **Dashboard**, **Environment**, **Operations**, **Planning**, **Alerts**, **Analysis**, and **Reports**. The previous screenshot shows us a snapshot of what's going on with the entire environment because we have the **World** object selected and we're currently under the **Dashboard** tab. If we were to select another object such as a host or VM, it would show us the same information particular to that object. The **Dashboard** tab is basically an overview of what our environment looks like. It shows the three major badges and the scores for the object. These are called widgets. Widgets are the objects that make up dashboards.

# The Environment tab

The Environment tab has four subtabs under it: **Overview**, **Scoreboard**, **Members**, and **Relationships**. As shown in the following screenshot, the **Overview** tab shows us all of the objects, sometimes called skittles, and their status according to the minor badge that is selected: **Health**, **Workload**, **Anomalies**, **Faults**, **Risk**, **Time**, **Capacity**, **Stress**, **Efficiency**, **Waste**, or **Density**.

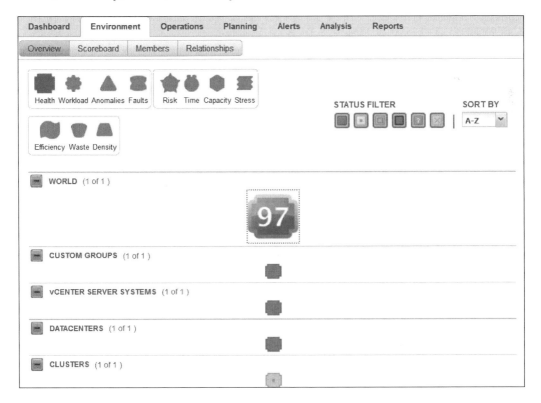

In this screenshot, **Health** is selected and we see a few green skittles and a yellow one next to **Clusters**. If we were to click on the **Workload** minor badge, then we would see the skittles change to reflect the workload scores for each object.

The **Scoreboard** tab gives us a lot of the same information in more detail. We can easily filter this view by clicking on the **FILTER OBJECTS** at the top.

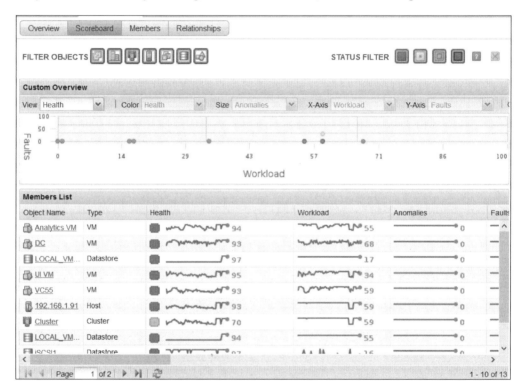

In the **Custom Overview**, we can select which major badge we'd like to show information for; in this case, **Health** is selected. On the vertical axis, we have **Anomalies** and on the horizontal axis is **Workload**. The little green circles represent objects within our environment that we can hover over and even click on to drill down into details about the object. Under the **Members List**, we see small graphs for each object and what their minor badge score is along with what it's looked like in the past. We can actually click on the objects here if we like. Doing this will take us to the **Operations** tab and show us the details for the object we clicked on.

Back on the **Environment** tab, we can click on the **Members** subtab. This lists the objects in the environment. It tells us what type of object it is, the parent object's name and type and, which policy it's assigned to. Recall from *Chapter 2, Installing vCenter Operations Manager*, we can create new policies and even modify the default policy.

Lastly, we have the **Relationships** subtab under the **Environment** tab. This is a really interesting picture of the environment because we can click on an object and see which other objects are directly related as well as see their statuses. In the following screenshot, I've selected a VM to show a more interesting view of the **Relationships** tab. Therefore, we can see it's in the **Discovered virtual machine** folder, which host it's on, and the two datastores it's connected to (datastore1 is the local datastore on the physical host).

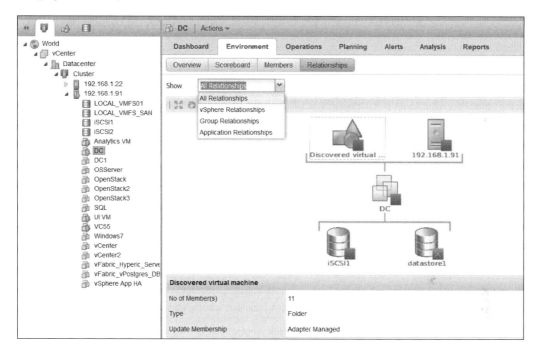

The previous screenshot shows that there's also a pull-down menu to select which view we'd like to see. Under the **Relationships** tab, we can also select one of the objects, as I've selected **Discovered virtual Machines**, and at the bottom, it shows us details for that object.

# The Operations tab

The Operations Tab has three subtabs: **Details**, **Events**, and **All Metrics**. By default, we see the **Details** tab that shows a detailed overview of the object's health. The **Operations** tab is highly geared toward the health of the objects in our environment and can be very helpful when we're trying to troubleshoot issues.

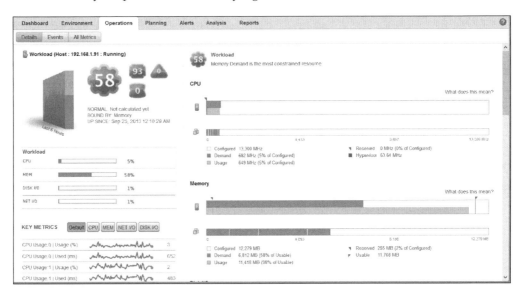

In the previous screenshot, we're looking at the details of a host within the environment. The top left section of the previous screenshot gives us an idea of the overall health of our host object. Currently, I've chosen the **Workload** badge so most of the information shown on the rest of the page is the **Workload** metrics for resources such as CPU, memory, and disk I/O. If I had selected one of the other badges, it would show me information on that. We can also get more details about key metrics by clicking on the buttons shown at the bottom left of the screenshot. By default, it shows **CPU** statistics, but I could click on the **MEM** button and get similar details about memory usage. If we were to scroll down, we'd see information for related objects. This is one of the first pages we'd look at if we suspected something was wrong with a particular host or VM. It gives us a very good idea of what's going on with that object. We would know right away if it didn't have enough memory because we'd see that the memory workload status was nearing or at 100%.

Next, we have the **Events** subtab shown as follows. The **Events** tab is just as the name suggests: it literally shows us events on the object we've selected (in this case a physical host) at the bottom of the screen. By default, these would be the events vCenter has generated. However, with other products from the vC Ops suite, such as vCenter Configuration Manager or Log Insight, we can see configuration changes to the guest operating system as well. We can also pick whether we'd like to see a graph representing **Health** in general, **Workload**, **Anomalies**, or **Faults**. The graph changes depending on what we've selected, the events are all the same.

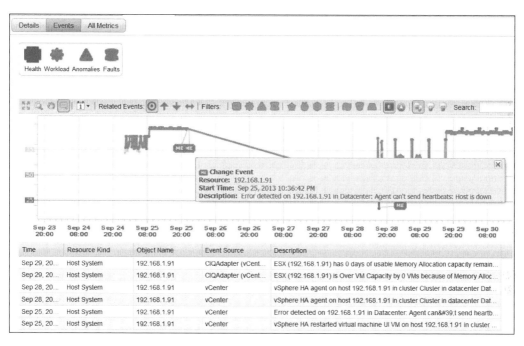

In the screenshot shown, I've hovered over the **Management Event** alert (**ME**) that shows a **Change Event**. In this case, the event is that I had shut down the physical host on September 25th at around 10 PM. We would also be able to see this event listed in the graph depicted in the following screenshot, which shows us how these events may have affected the host.

We then have the **All Metrics** subtab, which is pretty self-explanatory. It shows us pretty much anything and everything we could want. On the left, we use the **Metric Selector** to choose the metric we'd like to look at and on the right it shows us graphs correlating to that metric. The following screenshot shows some of the metrics available:

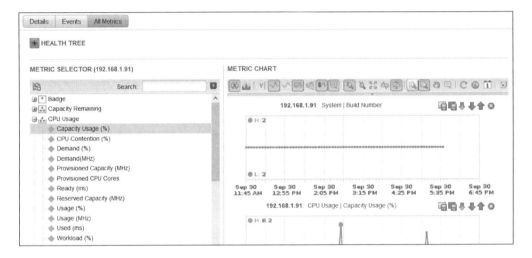

# The Planning tab

The **Planning** tab is really interesting. Again, we have three subtabs: **Summary**, **Views**, and **Events**. The information displayed here used to be available in an external application called CapacityIQ; however, since vC Ops has evolved, the planning functionality is also included within this dashboard. We can click on any object in our tree to see this information. In the following screenshot, I've selected the cluster level:

Under the **Objects** section, we see the **Trend and Forecast** graph as well as **Extended Forecast** and **Time Remaining**. As has been noted before, vC Ops learns our environments. So, if we're averaging adding a VM or two every week, it will learn that information and present us with a forecast that tells us how much capacity we have remaining. As we can see under **Time Remaining**, I have 29 days until I reach capacity within my cluster if I continue adding the same amounts of VMs. Keep in mind, if this is a new environment for us, the trending might change once this has all settled down. So, you want to keep vC Ops running and come back to it in a few weeks when it's learned that we're no longer moving at the same pace. In the **Resources** section, it will actually break down our time remaining by compute resources such as CPU and memory. This way, we'd be able to tell if we just need to add more memory.

The **Views** subtab allows us to look at specific things as well. For instance, we'd be able to break it down by **Time Remaining** or **Capacity**. We can even break it down by **Stress**, **Waste**, or **Density**. Under the **Events** subtab, we can see events related to when we added or removed compute resources. We can also change views here if we'd like to see graphs and events correlating with **Risk**, **Time**, **Capacity**, **Stress**, **Efficiency**, **Waste**, or **Density**.

# The Alerts tab

The **Alerts** tab shows us actual alerts for the objects we've chosen in the tree on the left. We can also navigate to this screen by clicking on the **Alerts** in the right pane of the vC Ops UI. See the following screenshot. It shows us how critical the alert is along with the resource that the alert refers to and a description of the alert.

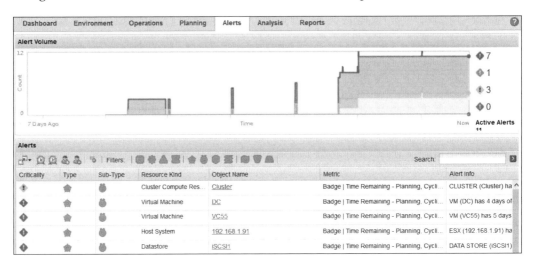

We might ask ourselves why we'd want to use these alerts when vCenter server gives us alerts as well. However, vCenter uses hard thresholds and doesn't know what's normal for a VM for instance. vCenter just lets us know if we're using 85% of our CPU. vC Ops will actually learn what our peak hours are, so it can let us know if for some reason our CPU utilization is high during a non-peak time. This information would be more helpful generally because it's anomalous behavior. This is what's known as *dynamic*, instead of static, *thresholding*.

# The Analysis tab

The **Analysis** tab lets us analyze various things depending on the object we've selected. It contains default descriptions we can click on to show us a heat map of what's going on within the environment. Let's look at the following screenshot to see what this means exactly:

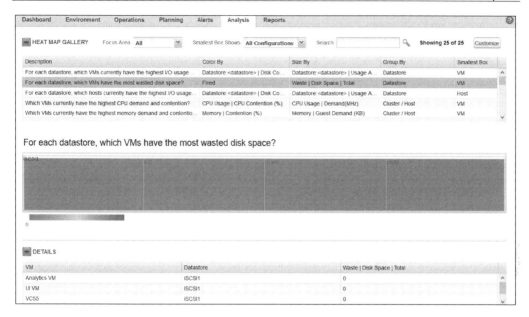

In the screenshot shown, I've selected the **Cluster** object on the left and chosen the **Description — For each datastore, which VMs have the most wasted disk space?**. The preceding heat map shows my datastore, iSCSI1, as well as three of my VMs. They're all green because I don't really have a lot of wasted space. I can choose any one of the default descriptions and if it applies to the object I have selected, it will show a heat map for that if applicable using the colors green, yellow, orange, and red. Green is basically good and red is bad. We can also click on the **Customize** button at the top right to create our own descriptions.

# The Reports tab

Finally, we have the **Reports** tab that contains several canned reports we can run. These can be scheduled to compile at a certain time or run on demand. Also, it gives us the option of a PDF or CSV file if we'd like to print out the information found in vC Ops for our manager, CIO, and others. These reports basically contain everything found in the other tabs, but make it easier to schedule, and perhaps send e-mails in an efficient way.

# Major badges

vC Ops uses badges to report on various aspects of how our environment is performing. There are three major badges that are made up of minor badges. The major badges are Health, Risk, and Efficiency. They can be green, yellow, orange, or red depending on the score we get in each category and the thresholds that are set up. Again, green is good and red is bad.

## The Health badge

The **Health** badge measures the health of our environment or an object within our environment. As depicted in the following screenshot, it will show us issues we may need to deal with immediately. It uses several advanced algorithms to calculate the minor badges that all come together to create the overall **Health** score. The minor badges associated with **Health** are **Workload**, **Anomalies**, and **Faults**.

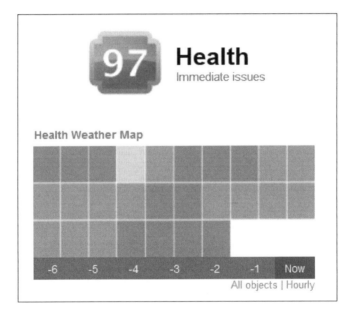

Under the **Dashboard** tab, we can see a quick view of how healthy our environment is now and for the last six hours. The weather map shows us objects within our environment. If we hover over one of the squares in the **Health Weather Map**, it will tell us the VM or host it is referring to. We can also double-click on the square to drill into that object and it takes us to the **Operations** tab under the **Details** subtab. If the box is gray, the object (VM) is probably off.

If we've selected a VM or something lower on the tree, to the left, it will show us a **Health Trend** graph instead of a weather map. This is displayed in the following screenshot. It still shows the health over the last six hours. According to this example, the health of my VM has been pretty close to 100 for the last six hours.

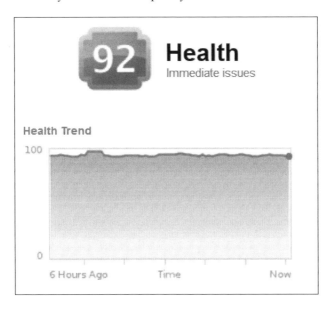

By default, if we have a score between 75 and 100, vC Ops considers the object to be normal and displays its score with a green background. If we have a health score of 50-74, there may be some problems and we're essentially being warned that we might need to pay attention to the object; it will appear yellow in the weather map. A score of 25-49 means it is getting worse and the health badge will be orange. Finally, a score under 25 is something we need to pay attention to immediately. The health badge will be red in this case.

We can get a low health score due to several reasons. For instance, the CPU utilization, memory utilization, or disk I/O might be way too high for too long. On the flip side, if our VMs are accustomed to this high utilization, and we experience a period of time where they aren't using the CPU, memory, or disk that they normally do, our health score could be lowered. Our networking might also be over utilized on the physical host. We could also be experiencing anomalous behavior such as high-memory utilization during an off-peak time. There could also be specific events or alerts that affect the health score such as HA not being configured, even though it's enabled or not receiving heartbeats on a host.

# The Risk badge

The **Risk** badge warns us of future issues. The scoring is the opposite of Health in that the lower score the better. By default, 0-49 means there aren't really problems in the future. The risk badge will be green in this case. Next, 50-74 means there may be potential for risk and 75-99 means risk is a little more imminent. If we have a score of 100, we are most likely to experience an issue in the near future. The minor badges associated with Risk are **Time Remaining**, **Capacity Remaining**, and **Stress**.

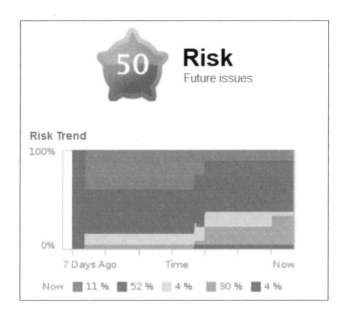

On the **Dashboard** tab, we will see the **Risk** widget as shown in the previous screenshot. It also gives us a quick view of the **Risk Trend** graph. The example shown in the previous screenshot is the **Risk Trend** graph for my **World** object. The graph shows the last seven days. As we can see in the previous example, my environment is experiencing more and more risk, most likely due to a lack of resources since this is my home lab. Much like the **Health** badge correlated with the **Operations** tab, the **Risk** badge correlates with the **Planning** tab. If we click on the **Risk** badge, it will take us directly to the **Views** subtab under the **Planning** tab.

What increases the risk score (that is, it's getting worse) is a lack of compute resources. This is not the same as the **Health** badge. The **Health** badge points to overutilization, which we can possibly fix by adding another vCPU or more RAM to a VM. The **Risk** badge points to actually running out of resources. If we only have 96 GB of RAM on our hosts and we're using more than that, the **Risk** badge will alert us to this. This applies to CPU, disk space, and networking bandwidth as well.

# The Efficiency Badge

The **Efficiency** Badge tells us whether we're using our resources in the most optimized way. Like the **Health** score, the higher the **Efficiency** score the better. If we have a score of 0, we're essentially wasting all our resources. It is most likely that all of the VMs are oversized. A score of 1-10 means we're still not utilizing all our resources like we should be and we should probably optimize more. A score of 11-25 is getting better, it means that the optimization is pretty good, but not great. A score over 25 is generally pretty good and nothing to be concerned about. The minor badges associated with the **Efficiency** badge are **Reclaimable Waste** and **Density**.

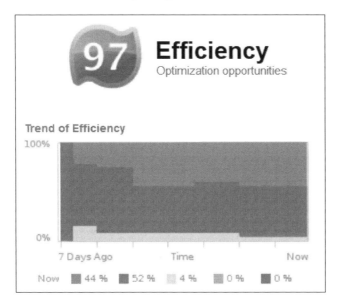

Back on the **Dashboard** page, we can see the **Efficiency** widget with a **Trend of Efficiency** graph for the last seven days. As we can see from the graph, most of my VMs are running pretty efficiently, meaning I don't have a lot of wasted resources. Clicking on the **Efficiency** badge or the **Trend of Efficiency** graph will also take us to the **Planning** tab under the **Views** subtab. However, by default, it selects the efficiency-related view **Capacity Efficiency**. If we're looking to find more information on efficiency, we can find it by going through the different views on the **Planning** tab.

# Minor badges

As noted in the *Major badges* section, there are several minor badges that make up each major badge and contribute to the total score for each major badge. The minor badges get their own scores as well to help narrow down where any issues are.

## The Workload badge

The **Workload** badge can be somewhat confusing. This metric doesn't just measure utilization, it checks many factors. It will check to see if there's a lot of resource contention and if objects are consistently vying for resources. It is a minor badge of the **Health** badge. When we click on the **Workload** badge, we're taken to the **Operations** tab under the **Details** subtab; but this time, we're shown the **Anomalies** view, which we can tell because the **Workload** badge is bigger than the other badges shown. It also reads **Workload** in the top left if we're not able to tell by the badge itself.

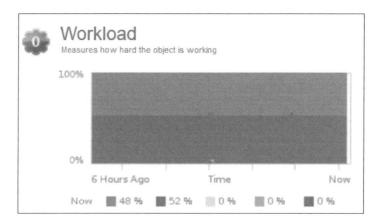

My **Workload** score above is 0 because nothing in my environment is working very hard. In this case, the lower the score the better. Although this also means we're not really using an object. If the **Workload** is high for an object, we'd want to check if maybe it's high during certain times. For instance, if we notice the workload is always high from midnight to 4:00 A.M., this might point toward our backups. If we're looking at a database server, maybe someone ran a query and we're able to narrow in and see that it's slowing down the VM.

# The Anomalies badge

As mentioned before, vC Ops learns our environment. It knows what's normal for a particular object and if it presents any anomalous behavior, this will be represented by the **Anomalies** score. This score is not based on absolutes because it's analyzing the trends in our environment. There really is no way to get this information without the use of vCenter Operations Manager. Again, the lower the score the better as it implies there aren't strange things going on within our environment. This is also a minor badge of the **Health** badge. When we click on the **Anomalies** tab, we are also taken to the **Operations** tab under the **Details** subtab and in this case, it shows us the **Anomalies** view.

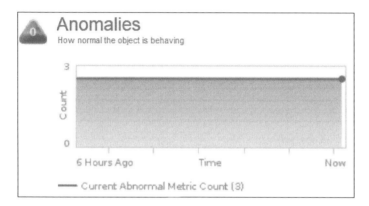

An example of using this would be finding a VM with a score above 75 and drilling into it. We might find that its memory usage is really high during a time that it normally has not been. At that point, we can narrow down the time period that it happened and see if we might be able to correlate it with a certain event. Perhaps, we'd find that it's related to an application upgrade on that VM and the new version has a bug that's causing a memory leak, and we can take action to remediate this issue.

# The Faults badge

The last of the minor badges under **Health**, the **Faults** badge, tells us about concrete events that our objects are experiencing. With the **Faults** badge, the lower the number the better.

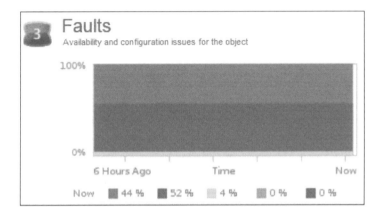

If we click on the **Faults** Badge, it will again take us to the **Operations** tab. Examples of what the **Faults** score is derived from are a power failure in the physical host or no NIC redundancy set up on our Management Network within vCenter. This badge is much less subjective than some of the other badges.

# The Time Remaining badge

The **Time Remaining** badge is exactly what it sounds like. It tells us how much time we have left for certain objects until we run out of resources or capacity. This is a minor badge of the **Risk** badge and contributes to the **Risk** score.

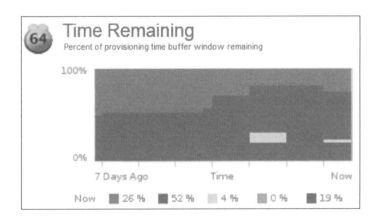

The way this score is generated is that it actually takes procurement time into account. By default, when the badge first turns red, it indicates we have 30 days left of whichever resource we're looking at. When we click on the **Time Remaining** badge, it takes us to the **Planning** tab and by default, shows us the **Virtual Machine Capacity** view as shown in the following screenshot:

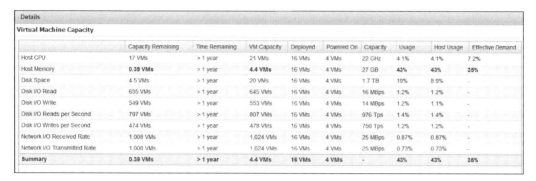

| Details | | | | | | | | | | |
|---|---|---|---|---|---|---|---|---|---|---|
| **Virtual Machine Capacity** | | | | | | | | | | |
| | Capacity Remaining | Time Remaining | VM Capacity | Deployed | Powered On | Capacity | Usage | Host Usage | Effective Demand |
| Host CPU | 17 VMs | > 1 year | 21 VMs | 16 VMs | 4 VMs | 22 GHz | 4.1% | 4.1% | 7.2% |
| Host Memory | **0.39 VMs** | > 1 year | **4.4 VMs** | 16 VMs | 4 VMs | 27 GB | 43% | 43% | 35% |
| Disk Space | 4.5 VMs | > 1 year | 20 VMs | 16 VMs | 4 VMs | 1.7 TB | 19% | 8.9% | - |
| Disk I/O Read | 635 VMs | > 1 year | 645 VMs | 16 VMs | 4 VMs | 16 MBps | 1.2% | 1.2% | - |
| Disk I/O Write | 549 VMs | > 1 year | 553 VMs | 16 VMs | 4 VMs | 14 MBps | 1.2% | 1.1% | - |
| Disk I/O Reads per Second | 797 VMs | > 1 year | 807 VMs | 16 VMs | 4 VMs | 976 Tps | 1.4% | 1.4% | - |
| Disk I/O Writes per Second | 474 VMs | > 1 year | 478 VMs | 16 VMs | 4 VMs | 750 Tps | 1.2% | 1.2% | - |
| Network I/O Received Rate | 1,008 VMs | > 1 year | 1,024 VMs | 16 VMs | 4 VMs | 25 MBps | 0.87% | 0.87% | - |
| Network I/O Transmitted Rate | 1,008 VMs | > 1 year | 1,024 VMs | 16 VMs | 4 VMs | 25 MBps | 0.73% | 0.73% | - |
| **Summary** | **0.39 VMs** | **> 1 year** | **4.4 VMs** | **16 VMs** | **4 VMs** | - | **43%** | **43%** | **35%** |

Using the previous shown chart, we can narrow down what we're low on. Since my **World** object is selected, it's showing me my time remaining for everything.

# The Capacity Remaining badge

The **Capacity Remaining** badge shows us how many more VMs we can fit in our environment. vC Ops figures out our average VM size, as well as the unused resources, and is able to tell us the capacity information. This minor badge also contributes to the **Risk** score.

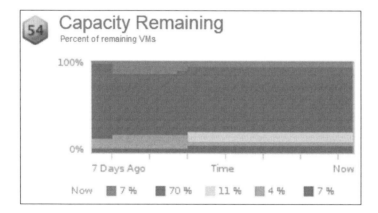

Something to keep in mind is that the calculations involved here really only include powered on VMs. If the VM is powered off the only thing considered is the storage used. The way the score is calculated is vC Ops figures out the limiting resources, for instance, if we're running out of disk space. It will then figure out how many VMs can fit in the remaining space. Then, it will divide the possible VMs by the total VMs (possible + current), which give us a percentage. This is where the score comes from. So, according to the previous score and graph, I can grow my environment more than 50 percent the size it is now. If we click on this badge, it will take us to the same place the **Time Remaining** badge takes us to get a break down by resource.

# The Stress badge

The **Stress** badge can be really helpful as it measure long-term workload. It tells us not only that our environment is stressed but also during which time periods it's stressed. This can be really helpful when troubleshooting. The **Stress** badge also contributes to the **Risk** score.

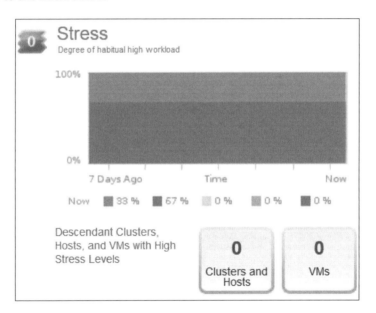

As shown in the previous screenshot, my environment is not very stressed. Note the description on this badge though. It says **Degree of habitual high workload**. So, this badge isn't showing us random peaks or one-off events, it's showing us when an object is stressed for a longer period of time. Again, this is different from workload because time is a more important factor. However, workload is definitely a factor of stress. Right on the widget, it also separates Clusters and Hosts from VMs and shows us how many of each are experiencing habitual stress.

An example of using the **Stress** badge would be if we're seeing some long-term stress on one of our hosts. Perhaps it's undersized for the amount of resources the VMs are taking up, but only on Fridays from 3:00 to 5:00 PM because that's when our DBA is running weekly reports. Now we know this is going to happen every Friday, so we can either accept that our other VMs on this host will run slower during this time, we can add resources to this host, or we can migrate VMs off this host to another less utilized host.

# The Reclaimable Waste badge

The **Reclaimable Waste** badge is really interesting because it's part of the **Efficiency** score and most people would agree that if vC Ops can save them from having to purchase more resources, then that's pretty great. **Reclaimable Waste** lets us know that we have oversized VMs and therefore, how many resources we can reallocate to new VMs. The **Reclaimable Waste** widget shows us the percentage of our total capacity that can be reclaimed and then breaks it down by **vCPU**, **Disk**, and **Memory**.

While the **Reclaimable Waste** widget shows us all this information, and we can also click on the badge to be taken to the **Planning** tab, we really need to go through the Oversized and Undersized VMs report to figure out where these resources are assigned. To get a better **Reclaimable Waste** score, we can then take some of the resources that aren't being used on the current VMs and put them back in our pool for new VMs. However, we do need to keep in mind that vC Ops is using a best guess here. There may be VMs that we only use seasonally or something along those lines, which vC Ops may see as waste. It's always a good idea to think through the usage of the VM logically before we start reclaiming waste.

# The Density badge

The **Density** badge is the last of the minor badges and it is also a part of the **Efficiency** score. Understanding the **Density** score can be more difficult because people confuse it with **Reclaimable Waste**. However, density actually measures how much we can consolidate resources without experiencing performance hits. Whereas the **Reclaimable Waste** badge just tells us how VMs are oversized. If we think about it, the term *density* really makes sense because it asks how many objects can we fit inside my environment? If we have a score of over 25, then we have a pretty good consolidation ratio.

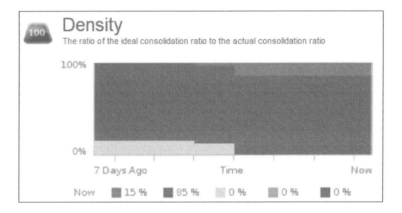

This can also show us where we might have some cost savings opportunity. If I can fit more objects in my environment without causing performance issues, this widget will give me an idea of that. To give a more specific example of how the **Density** badge works, we need to consider CPU contention. Although we can overcommit CPU with VMware, we might start to experience CPU contention, especially if more than one vCPU is assigned to a VM. Density will let us know that CPU contention might become an issue or perhaps already is.

Keep in mind that the efficiency-related scores can also take into account usable capacity. This means if we have HA configured, it can be included in the calculation and, therefore, not counted as usable resources.

**Usable capacity**

Configure usable capacity thresholds.

Usable Capacity settings are only applied to Time Remaining metrics if the basis for Capacity Remaining on  Capacity & Time Remaining  tab is set to **Usable Capacity**.

**Usable Capacity Rules**

☑ Use High Availability (HA) configuration, and reduce capacity

☐ % of CPU capacity to reserve as buffer:     `10`  %

☐ % of Memory capacity to reserve as buffer:     `10`  %

☐ % of Disk I/O capacity to reserve as buffer:     `10`  %

☐ % of Disk Space capacity to reserve as buffer:     `10`  %

☐ % of Network I/O capacity to reserve as buffer:   `10`  %

**Capacity Calculation Rules**

◉ Use last known capacity

○ Use actual capacity

# Heat maps

**Heat maps** are used to show how objects are doing relative to each other and sometimes relative to time. I mentioned heat maps in the *Analysis* section earlier in this chapter, but it's worth going into how to read heat maps and also creating our own.

When we're in the regular UI of vC Ops and we click on **Analysis**, we can choose different heat maps we'd like to see. Let's look at an example to get a clearer understanding of how heat maps work.

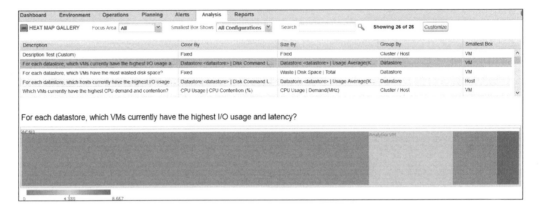

In the previous screenshot, I've chosen the heat map **For each datastore, which VMs currently have the highest IO usage and latency?**. We can see how this heat map is configured by looking under the **Color By**, **Fixed**, **Cluster/Host**, and **Smallest Box** columns. Let's take a closer look at how this is configured by clicking on the **Customize** button and selecting this **Description**. That shows us the following configuration:

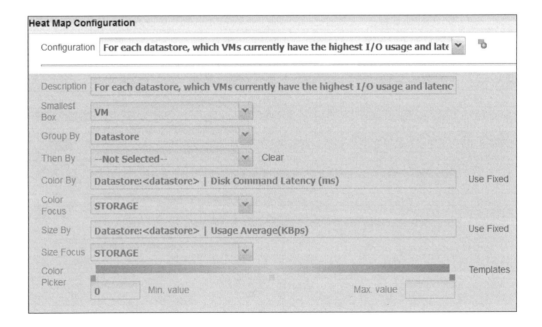

The **Smallest Box** dropdown can be used to specify what type of vSphere object we want the heat map to display. Usually, this is a VM because it is a *smaller* object that doesn't really contain other objects, at least as far as vC Ops goes. Since this is a **For each datastore** description, we'll be grouping by datastore. Obviously, if this were a **For each host** description, we would group by host and so on. We can also group by a second category if we like. The **Color By** category, in this case, is determined by **Disk Command Latency**. The color focus is obviously storage because we're dealing with datastores' IO and latency. Now we're going to size the boxes by usage. As we can see, the UI VM is not the highest IO usage because it's smaller than the other boxes, but it does have the highest latency because it's red. We can also create custom heat maps if there's something we'd like to see that isn't included. Perhaps we'd like to show CPU usage along with amount of CPU cores. There are other ways we can group things, such as by SLA or application, or perhaps even better, by user-defined group.

It's also worth noting that we have heat maps in our custom UI, which again we get to by going to `https://<IP_Address_UI_VM>/vC Ops-custom`. Go to the **Heatmaps** tab and we'll see several preconfigured heat maps there as shown in the following screenshot. I've also shown the options available in the pull-down menus.

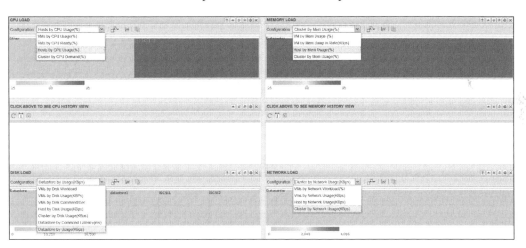

We can edit and do many of the same things with these heat maps as we can with the heat maps in the regular UI.

# Custom dashboards

While we're still in the custom UI let's talk about creating custom dashboards. This option is only available to those with a vC Ops Enterprise license. Again, to get to the custom dashboards, we need to open the custom UI at `https://<IP_address_UI_VM>/vC Ops-custom`. If we hover over the **DASHBOARDS** option on the top left, we get a few new options. Click on **Add a dashboard** to create a new dashboard.

This brings us to **DASHBOARD EDITING**. We can drag the widgets on the left over to the right to add them to our new custom dashboard as shown in the following screenshot:

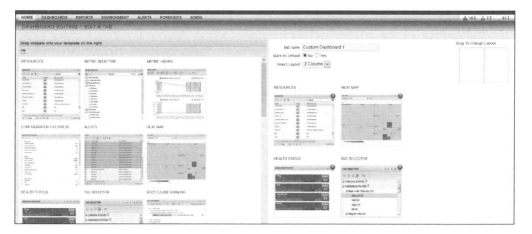

We can also name the tab, mark it as default, and select the layout columns. At the top right, we can also change how the columns are sized. Once we click on **OK**, we have our new dashboard.

Keep in mind we can also group items, search for them, and even add them to our custom dashboards by creating and assigning resource tags to our objects. Suppose we have a lot of dev servers, even hosts, clusters, and datastores that are specifically for our dev/QA department. One way to group all these things together is by using resource tags in our custom UI.

Use the following steps to create a tag:

1. Hover over the **Environment** tab.
2. Click on **Environment View**.
3. Select the **Manage Tags** icon (fourth from the left) in the left pane.

4. Click on the **Add Tag** icon.

5. Enter a name for the tag.

6. Now on the right-hand side, type in a value for the tag. The value would be an individual object within this tag, such as server names and datastore names. There is the possibility to have multiple values.

7. Now click on **OK**.

8. Once the tag is created, it will appear on the left-hand side with the other default tags.

9. Drag and drop any appropriate object from the right pane into this **Tag** container.

# Summary

This chapter had a lot of information in it, but all of it is absolutely necessary for understanding vCenter Operation Manager. We went over the various tabs offered in both the regular UI and custom UI of vC Ops. Using these tabs, we got a general overview of our environment through the Dashboard and Environment tabs, and a more detailed view of any issues within our environment through the Operations tab and of capacity planning and issues through the Planning and Analysis tabs. We can also see specific alerts and create reports by going to the Alerts tab and get reports by going to the Reports tab.

vC Ops gives us a great way to see at a glance goings-on with the use of major badges—Health, Risk, and Efficiency—as well as more of an in-depth view using the minor badges—Workload, Anomalies, Faults, Time Remaining, Capacity Remaining, Stress, Reclaimable Waste, and Density. These minor badges fall under the major badges and give us scores so we can see how our environment is doing from day to day or at any given time we look at vC Ops.

We then dove into more specifics about heat maps and how they show us objects' resource usage as compared to other objects. We saw how we can create custom heat maps as well. Heat maps are also present in the vC Ops custom UI, where we can customize them as well. As if that's not enough customization, we then went on to create custom dashboards, only available in the Enterprise version. We can use custom dashboards to see the metrics we care about the most and grouped together on one tab.

In the next chapter, we'll get into using vC Ops for some real troubleshooting. It will have several examples of how we can find problems and alleviate them, then hopefully take actions to prevent them from happening again.

# 4
# Troubleshooting Our Virtual Environment with vCenter Operations Manager

We'll cover the following topics in this chapter:

- Drilling in on major and minor badges
- Troubleshooting VM performance
- Troubleshooting network performance
- Troubleshooting slow applications
- Finding future risks

The core uses for vC Ops are *troubleshooting* and *capacity planning* within our virtual environment. In this chapter, we'll concentrate on the former. Troubleshooting can be confusing in vC Ops as there is just so much information within it that it can be overwhelming and somewhat intimidating. What has helped me is keeping in mind that there's not necessarily one right way to get our answers. Essentially, we shouldn't feel like we're going about something the wrong way; we should feel free to explore the UI and get as much information as we can. Also, as we all know, there can be multiple contributing factors to issues within our environments, so again feel free to explore! In this chapter, we will see some practical examples of how to troubleshoot specific scenarios. This will give us an idea of how to go about it and also help us familiarize ourselves with the UI. The content in the previous chapter will also be a big help in understanding how to navigate throughout the various displays that vC Ops offers.

# Drilling in on major and minor badges

Let's look at the **Dashboard** tab once again. This gives us a broad idea of what's going on in our environment. This can be really helpful for maintaining our environment. We don't need the best scores on all the badges, but it definitely looks a little nicer when everything is green. Due to resource constraints, budgetary issues, and other business issues we may not be able to get to a score of 100 for health and 0 for risk. As long as it's in the green, we should feel pretty good about our environment, though. If the **Health** badge isn't green, we can click on the arrow next to **Why is Health 55?**

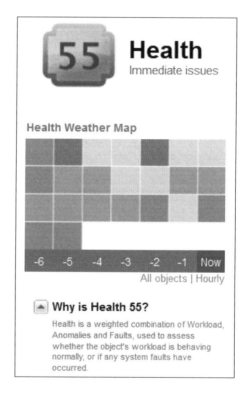

This will show what the minor badge scores are. We can get an idea from this as to what is causing our **Health** score to be so much lower than it should be. These examples are for the entire environment as we are getting a broad look at what's going on. I can also select an object within my environment and get the same information at a more detailed level.

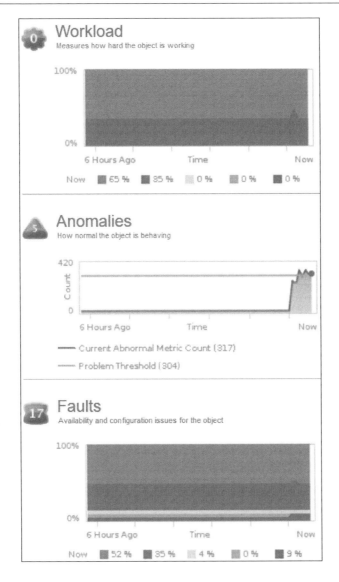

If our Workload badge appears high, we can quickly draw the conclusion that our environment is working hard based on the resources available. If we also check the **Stress** badge and see a high number there while the **Anomalies** badge is low, this would indicate that the workload is consistently high and has been for a while. These numbers most likely an indication that we need to add resources to our environment. This begs the question as to whether we need to add memory, CPU, networking resources, storage, or perhaps all of these peripherals. We can alleviate workload and stress by adding another physical host to our cluster, but this could be overkill.

Now if our **Workload** score is high along with our **Anomalies** score, there is most likely something out of the ordinary going on in our environment. Maybe someone changed a limit or reservation in a resource pool, or someone has upgraded the VMware Tools without testing and the upgrade has bugs. If the **Faults** score is high on top of this, then we need to really dive in and see what's going on. From my previous example we're not seeing too many problems with the **Workload**. In fact all of my badges are green, but I am seeing some anomalous behavior and faults.

Let's take a look at the **Environment** tab to get a more detailed view of what's going on. Again, we're still just getting an idea of how our environment looks; we're not troubleshooting a specific issue at this point.

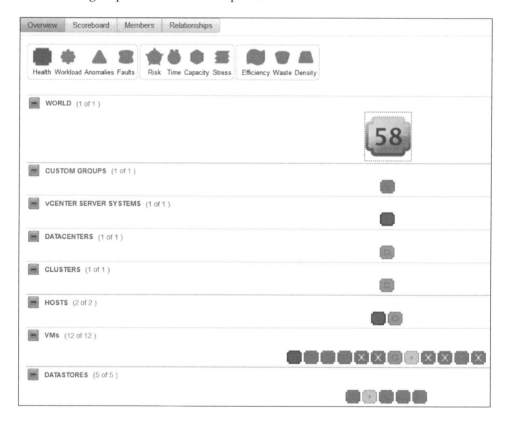

As discussed in the previous chapter, the **Environment** tab shows us a view of the skittles representing our objects for every major and minor badge depending on what we click on. The previous example shows us the health of our environment. We have a few red and orange skittles that are concerning and that contribute to our **Health** score not being great. The first red skittle is our **vCenter Server System**. If we double-click on that skittle it takes us to the **Operations** tab for vCenter specifically.

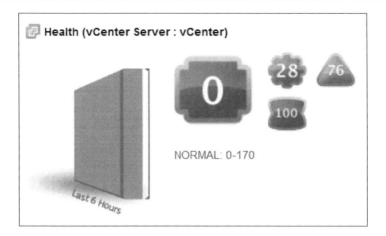

From our previous example, we see the **Health** badge, which is the bigger badge, and then the three minor badges. **Workload** has a score of 28 and is green; **Anomalies** has a score of 76 and is orange; and **Faults** shows 100 and is red. If we go ahead and click on the **Faults** badge, we can see that the Faults badge becomes the focus in the upper-left widget, and it lists any faults we have on our vCenter server.

We'll want to research the error and see if we can correct it. In this case, according to VMware KB 2015763 (`http://kb.vmware.com/selfservice/microsites/search.do?language=en_US&cmd=displayKC&externalId=2015763`) we can safely ignore this error. Once we correct the error, we can wait for it to clean up, or we can press the icon next to **Alert Information**, which lets us cancel the fault. If we haven't corrected the error, it will reappear again later.

Now let's click on the **Anomalies** badge. We can see all the anomalous behavior for the vCenter server. It shows a break down on the widget on the right-hand side:

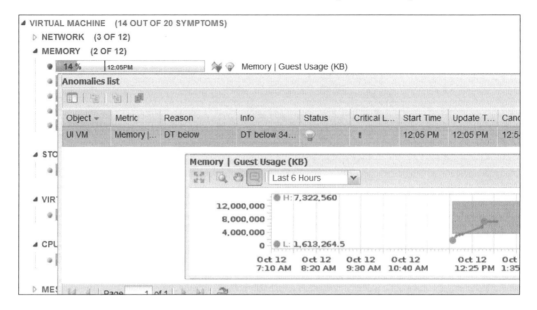

When we click on an **arrow** next to one of our resources, such as **Memory**, it shows us some of the anomalous behaviors vCenter memory has experienced. If we hover over the **graph** icon next to the status bars, it tells us whether it has been above or below the dynamic threshold. Again the dynamic threshold has been learned by vC Ops. If we hover over the **light bulb** icon, it tells us if this is actively happening right now. In the previous example, I've double-clicked on the **Memory | Guest Usage** status bar, which brings up a pop-up called **Anomalies List**. This list tells us the following specifics about each anomaly for each object. The first object in the list is for the UI VM because we're at the top level of vCenter or rather still looking at the entire site managed by this vCenter. As we can see, the anomalous behavior is no longer currently active because the light bulb is not yellow. It only has a criticality level of *warning*, and it started at 12:05 PM on October 12. If we double-click on the list item, another pop-up is shown, which is the graph of **Memory | Guest Usage (KB)**. The area in gray shows us what's normal for this VM while the blue line shows the actual usage. The orange dots are the low and high values, and the actual numbers of the low and high values are shown on the left-hand side. In this case, we're not too worried about this anomalous behavior because it's no longer anomalous and was most likely down to the fact that I had just started that VM as the line starts right around 12:05 PM.

Let's look at another example. One of the host skittles was red as well. We'll start by clicking on that skittle and then selecting the **Relationships** tab.

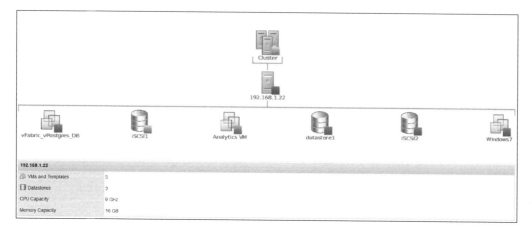

We can see here if there are other contributing factors as to why our host has a bad health score. We could also see if perhaps it's affecting our VMs for instance. If all of our VMs were showing red, we might need to be concerned. Since only a couple aren't showing green, it doesn't look like the host is affecting the performance of the VMs too much. So let's go ahead and drill into the host by selecting it in the tree on the left-hand side pane and go back to the **Operations** tab.

On the left-hand side, we see **Key Metrics** for the CPU, memory, network, and disk I/O. If we select **CPU**, we see the graphs shown in the following screenshot:

| KEY METRICS | Default CPU MEM NET I/O DISK I/O | |
| --- | --- | --- |
| CPU Usage \| CPU Contention (%) | | 0.54 |
| CPU Usage \| Workload (%) | | 2 |
| CPU Usage \| Demand(MHz) | | 211 |
| CPU Usage \| Usage (MHz) | | 196 |

The CPU usage looks pretty good because it's all within the normal range, which is actually pretty low. If we hover over or click on the numbers to the right, we can see full graphs with more details, which give us the low and high values again. Since the CPU looks good let's take a look at the memory.

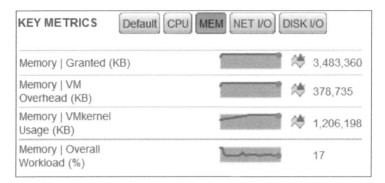

The memory graphs aren't looking as good. The graph next to it is showing that memory has been above the dynamic threshold. Our initial thoughts would be that we need to alleviate the memory usage, which we can simply do by adding more memory. Is this absolutely necessary, though? Well, let's take a look at the major and minor **Risk** badges to see what we can find there.

We'll go back to the **Dashboard** tab and then click on the **Risk** badge, which takes us to the **Planning** tab. We could of course also just click on the **Planning** tab to begin with and find the **View** that we're looking for. As I said in the beginning of this chapter, there are many different ways to navigate through vCenter Operations Manager. If we do get here by clicking on the **Risk** badge, it takes us to the **Virtual Machine Capacity** view.

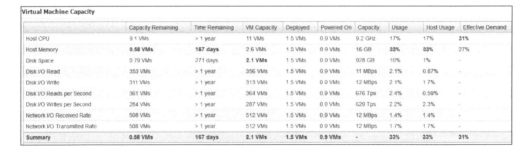

Virtual Machine Capacity

| | Capacity Remaining | Time Remaining | VM Capacity | Deployed | Powered On | Capacity | Usage | Host Usage | Effective Demand |
|---|---|---|---|---|---|---|---|---|---|
| Host CPU | 9.1 VMs | > 1 year | 11 VMs | 1.5 VMs | 0.9 VMs | 9.2 GHz | 17% | 17% | 31% |
| Host Memory | 0.58 VMs | 167 days | 2.6 VMs | 1.5 VMs | 0.9 VMs | 16 GB | 33% | 33% | 27% |
| Disk Space | 0.79 VMs | 271 days | 2.1 VMs | 1.5 VMs | 0.9 VMs | 928 GB | 10% | 1% | - |
| Disk I/O Read | 353 VMs | > 1 year | 356 VMs | 1.5 VMs | 0.9 VMs | 11 MBps | 2.1% | 0.87% | - |
| Disk I/O Write | 311 VMs | > 1 year | 313 VMs | 1.5 VMs | 0.9 VMs | 12 MBps | 2.1% | 1.7% | - |
| Disk I/O Reads per Second | 361 VMs | > 1 year | 364 VMs | 1.5 VMs | 0.9 VMs | 676 Tps | 2.4% | 0.59% | - |
| Disk I/O Writes per Second | 284 VMs | > 1 year | 287 VMs | 1.5 VMs | 0.0 VMs | 629 Tps | 2.2% | 2.3% | - |
| Network I/O Received Rate | 508 VMs | > 1 year | 512 VMs | 1.5 VMs | 0.9 VMs | 12 MBps | 1.4% | 1.4% | - |
| Network I/O Transmitted Rate | 508 VMs | > 1 year | 512 VMs | 1.5 VMs | 0.9 VMs | 12 MBps | 1.7% | 1.7% | - |
| **Summary** | **0.58 VMs** | **167 days** | **2.1 VMs** | **1.5 VMs** | **0.9 VMs** | **-** | **33%** | **33%** | **31%** |

We can see under **Capacity Remaining** that we only have enough memory for about a half of a VM. vC Ops considers the average size of our VMs to do this calculation. It also shows that we have about 167 days left with our current memory resources. Again, it's using historical data and how our environment is used to calculate this number as well. At the bottom of the graph, we see **Summary**, which takes the lowest values from the graph. For the most part, **Host Memory** has proven to be our bottleneck.

We've looked at the entire environment, and we've looked at a single host. Let's dive into storage a little bit by looking at a datastore. To get to our datastores easily, just click on the **Datastores** icon in the left-hand side pane. Then expand the **Datacenter** object to see all our datastores. In the following example, I selected my datastore named iSCSI1 and clicked on the **Health** badge, which took me to the **Operations** tab. I then selected the **Workload** badge to see the following graphs:

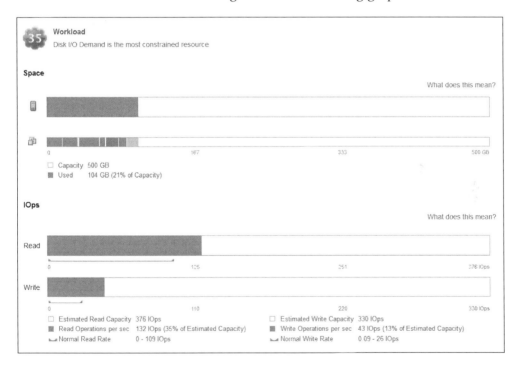

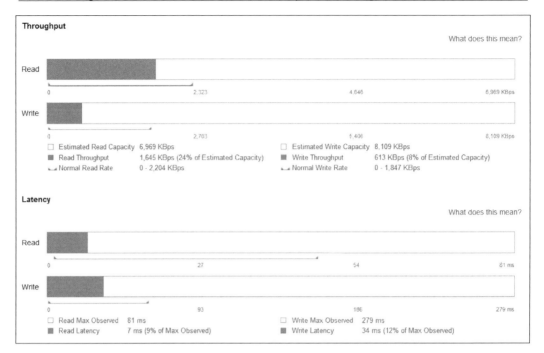

The first pair of graphs, **Space**, shows us physical space on our datastore. As shown, I've used 104 GB and have 500 GB in total. The second graph of the first pair also breaks it down by VM. If I hover over each box, it will tell me which VM the box represents and how much space it's taking up. It also shows the **Disk Workload** data for that VM.

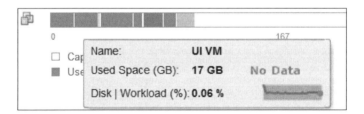

Let's move down to the **IOps** graphs. Here we're shown a **Read** and **Write** graph with the number of read IOps and write IOps we're actually using as well as the estimated capacity for both. The blue line underneath shows us what's normal for this environment. If we were to click on the **What does this mean?** link, it tells us that it compares the current operations per second to the estimated capacity and the normal rate for both reads and writes.

Though it's outside of the scope of this book to go into a deep dive on IOps, it's important to understand what they are from a high level. IOps, sometimes IOPS, stands for input/output operations per second. The most basic definition is that they are the measurement of reads from and writes to our storage.

The **Throughput** graphs show the number of KB read or written per second, also known as disk I/O. Again, we are shown what our current throughput is and the estimated maximum. The graph in the previous example shows that we are within our normal range as of now.

Finally the **Latency** graph shows us how quickly we're able to find the information we need on the disks. According to the link, we are told "The Latency section compares the current Latency to Max Observed and Normal Latency for both reads and writes."

If we're seeing high numbers for any of these graphs, we may want to consider using **Storage vMotion** for moving some of our VMs to another datastore. If we are having similar problems with our other datastores, then it might be time to consider buying more disks.

At the bottom of the page, we have a **Storage** section that shows us the **LUN** name as well as some other useful details.

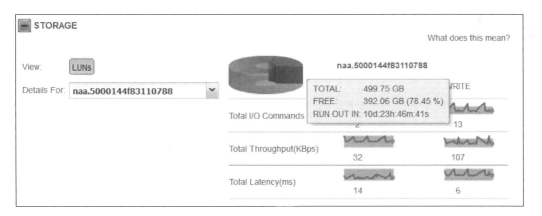

# Troubleshooting VM performance

A lot of times, we actually know that a certain object, perhaps a VM, is performing poorly, but we may not know why. vCenter Operations Manager can help us find the issue, so we can hopefully correct it. In the example shown as follows, my SQL server is slow. The first thing I'm going to do is jump on the vC Ops UI by opening a browser and navigating to `https://<vcops_IP_address>/vcops-vsphere` to check out the **Dashboard** tab for that particular VM.

>  We can search for the VM in the upper-right corner if we don't want to deal with expanding the tree and searching through all of the VMs in our environment.

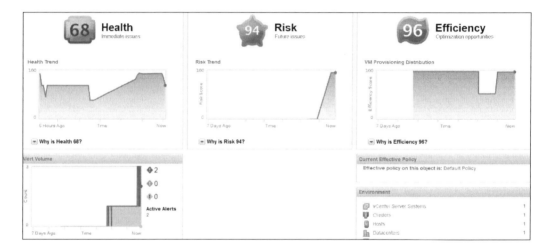

We see immediately that the **Health** score isn't great, and the **Risk** score is even worse. There are also a couple of **Active Alerts** that we could check out. Where do we begin? I would start by drilling into the **Health** badge because that relates to issues that are going on right now. This could be an issue that happens daily, weekly, or maybe has been happening consistently for a while, which **Risk** can tell us about, but we want to see what's going on currently first.

If we double-click on the **Health** badge, we see a screen similar to the one shown in the following screenshot:

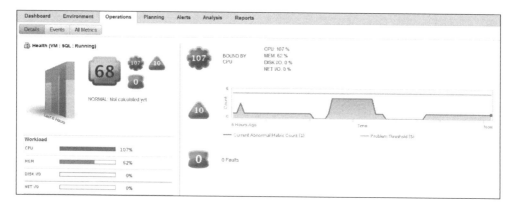

 How can the Workload score be 107? We can see the workload score at 100, as shown previously, when a VM is trying to use more resources than it's been given access to. If this is something that we see consistently, we need to allocate more resources to the physical host and/or VM.

The **Workload** score jumps out at us right away. The badge is red and has a score of 107. I can also see in the following graphs that the CPU load is 107 percent, and the memory is getting up there at 62 percent as well. Since this is a new VM in my environment, it hasn't yet been able to calculate the norm yet, so we don't see any blue lines showing us that the norm is below the **Workload** graphs. We also see the message **NORMAL: Not calculated yet**. If a VM in our environment has been running for a while, we will see these statistics in there. At this point, let's click on the **Workload** badge to see what else we can find.

We're seeing a lot more red in this section. Here, we can see the actual numbers when it comes to CPU usage. This VM is entitled to 3.325 MHz, but the demand is more than that at 3.558 MHz, which is 107 percent of the available CPU. We can also see that there is no reservation configured on this VM.

At this point, we'd like to see more details. The best troubleshooters in technology always begin with a single, simple question—what has changed? So, if we click on the **Events** sub tab, we can at least find out when this started happening, which can help us narrow down the possibilities with respect to what has changed.

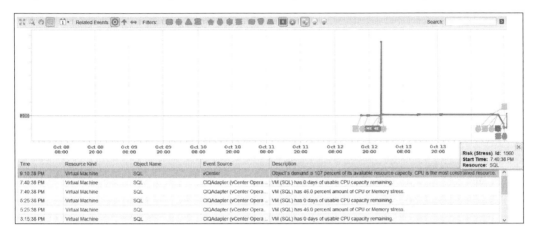

Around 7:40 PM, we see that the CPU started going up. It says it's using about 46 percent of the CPU or memory. Around 9:10 PM, we see that it's at 107 per cent usage. So, we need to ask our database administrator or Windows administrator what happened around 7:30 PM. Was there a SQL query run? Did someone do an upgrade? Did someone add a new database? Also notice that the graph is red and that the CPU has been running at 100-plus per cent for several days. At the end of the graph it went green and dipped lower. Then it started spiking again. So, we can also ask what happened at the time when the CPU usage dipped.

Here's a flowchart showing the first part of the troubleshooting. This shows what I described previously but might clear up the navigation.

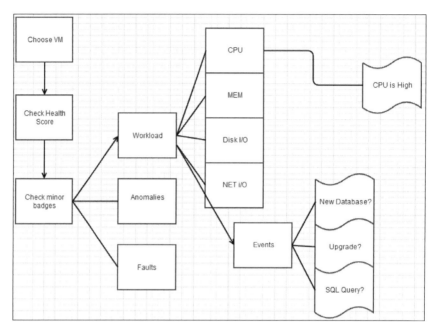

Let's go back to our dashboard to see how else we can track this problem. If we click on the **Active Alerts**, it shows us the following graph:

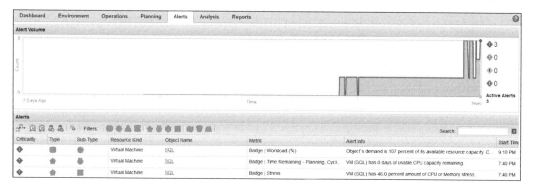

This gives us pretty similar information quickly. However, it doesn't give us the CPU details we might need if it were a different issue. Again though, we see around 7:40 PM that the CPU usage is starting to spike and then at 9:10 PM that it's at 107 per cent. We can double-click on these alerts to get more detailed information as well.

Let's go back to the **Dashboard** for our SQL VM one more time. Notice that the **Risk** score is really high. Let's drill into that to find out more information.

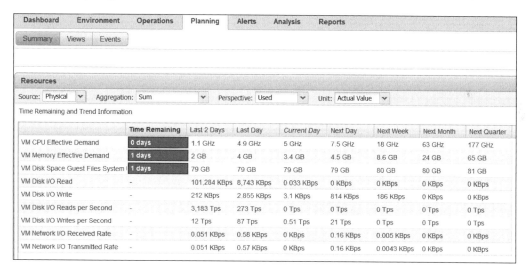

We're taken to the **Planning** tab, and we see in red that we have 0 days remaining of **VM CPU Effective Demand** and only 1 day remaining of **VM Memory Effective Demand**. The disk space isn't looking too good either, but that's just because this is a smaller VM, and we have a lot on it. We're also shown that two days ago we were only using 1.1 GHz on average of CPU Effective Demand. The day before we were using 4.9 GHz on average, and today we're up to 5 GHz. vC Ops gives us projections of the amount of demand we'll be using tomorrow, next week, next month, and so on. If we keep going this way, and the VM is supposed to be using this amount of CPU, then we will obviously need to add more compute resources. If we click on the **Events** sub tab, we get information similar to the events shown under the **Operations** tab when we clicked on the **Health** badge.

After asking our database administrator about it, we realize that he added another database that was just too much load for this VM. He transferred it to another SQL server, and only five minutes later, the CPU usage on vC Ops jumps down, and we see the **Health** and **Workload** scores start to improve. In a few more minutes, it is likely that all of the badges will be shown in green.

Let's take a look at another example. Our **vFabric Hyperic Server** that we use to monitor services is having a lot of issues. We constantly need to restart it, and since it's a virtual appliance and uses a Linux kernel, we can't easily see what's going on within the VM. Sometimes we can't even get to the web UI. Let's follow the same process that we did with the last example. If we click on the vFabric Hyperic server in the tree on the left-hand side, we see the **Dashboard** tab and find that the **Health** score is falling. The next step is to drill into **Health**.

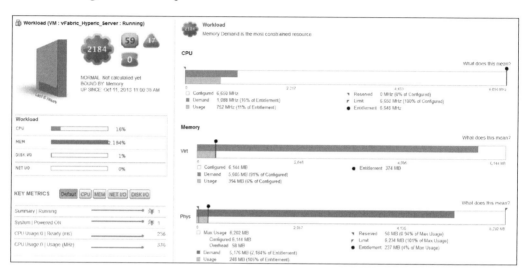

We're surprised to see that **Workload** is at 2184! When we check how much memory is assigned to the VM, we see the following under **Edit Settings** from the vSphere client.

It looks like we've given it about 6 GB of RAM, and we don't see a limit specified. It's hard to believe that we need 2184 percent more RAM than 6 GB, though. When we go back to our vSphere client, we notice that our vFabric Hyperic server is actually part of a vApp. Let's check the settings on that vApp:

Here's the issue. Sure enough, there's a limit specified of 632 MB. One of the junior admins had just learned about reservations and limits and was testing it out; unfortunately they assigned the limit to the wrong VM. Once we take away that limit, our **Health** scores will return to normal. Also, if this had been a regular VM, we would have seen the limit directly from the vC Ops **Operations** tab.

# Troubleshooting network performance

In this example, we have another slow VM. The SQL server is acting up again, but the DBA says they haven't been running anything out of the ordinary on it. So again we search for our SQL VM at the top-right in the vC Ops UI. We see **Health** has degraded, so we drill into the **Health** badge right away, and we see screen shown in the following screenshot:

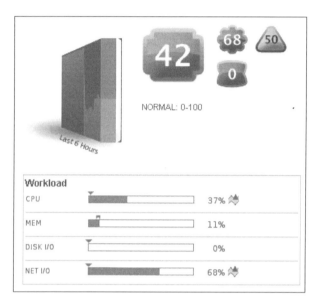

We can see that the **NET I/O** is the biggest bottleneck here. The graph to the next of it shows that we are over our dynamic threshold, which is usually around 1 percent, as shown by the arrow on top of the graph. Since this is a VM, it's pretty reasonable to wonder if only this VM or the actual host is experiencing the issue. So we scroll down towards the bottom of the page to see **Related Objects**. The **Parent Object**, which is the physical host, is being shown as green, with a **Health** score of 79, so it is most likely that the network I/O issue is only with our SQL VM.

If we scroll all the way down, we can expand our **Network Interface** section.

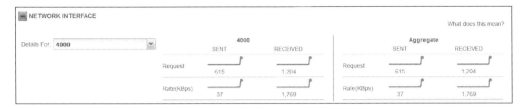

We can select what we'd like to see the **Details For**. The **4000**, as shown, shows us the statistics for the virtual NIC, but we can also select one of the physical NICs. If we check all the physical NICs, we might see that there's a problem with just one of them and narrow down the issue that way. If we are only experiencing the issue with a particular VM, it might be a driver issue or perhaps we simply need to install VMware Tools. If we're seeing issues with a few VMs, perhaps there is a problem with just one of the physical NICs we have assigned to that vSwitch. At that point, we need to start finding similarities between the VMs with the network issues. If we're seeing a problem with the host, it may be that there's a problem with an entire network card, NIC drivers on the host, or even that a physical connection was disconnected. It could also just be that it's lunch time, and too many people are watching Netflix.

# Troubleshooting slow applications

In *Chapter 3*, *Dashboards and Badges*, I described a concept called groups. We can create groups in the normal UI as well as in the custom UI that comes with the Enterprise version. There are default categories for groups, and these are **Department**, **Environment**, **Folder**, **Function**, **Location**, **Security Zone**, and **Service Level Objective**. To manually create a group of VMs that contain different parts of an application, we can create groups of these servers and see aggregate **Health**, **Risk**, and **Efficiency** scores. This makes it a lot easier to troubleshoot application issues than searching each VM individually and hoping we don't forget one. For example, we can put our vCenter server VM as well as the SQL server that holds the vCenter database in there. We could also create a group for any server within a vApp.

To create a group, use the following steps:

1. Click on the **Add Group** icon at the bottom-left in the left-hand side pane.

2. Give our group a **Name**, **Description** (optional), assign it a **Type**, configure how it gets its **Policy**, and then select **Membership Type**. If we choose **Dynamic**, we can configure rules to automatically have VMs put in the group, or we can choose **Manual** to create the list ourselves.

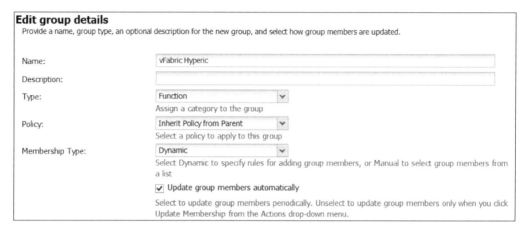

3. On the next page, we define the membership. We can specify search criteria, such as **Datastore** or **Host**. We can also add objects or exclude them here.

4. Then we review our settings and click on **Finish**.

Now we can see data for all the objects we've put in our group. In this case my vFabric Hyperic servers. The weather map under **Health** shows us all the VMs and how they're doing. As we can see from my example, one of the VMs is yellow and one is green:

Other examples of groups would be application servers and SQL servers. We should even consider the familiar VMware servers and put them in a group. Perhaps we'd like to see our vCenter server, database server(s), web server(s), and SSO server(s) in the same group. This could be handy when the management of vSphere seems a little slow or if you can't get to it at all.

# Finding future risks

With future risks, we don't necessarily know where we need to start looking because, right now, everything is seemingly okay. In this case, we can go to the **Dashboard** tab of our World or vCenter object and see what the **Risk** score is, or we can go ahead and click on our **Environment** tab. In the **Environment** tab, we'll select the **Risk** badge or the **Time**, **Capacity**, or **Stress**, minor badges to see where we might have some issues.

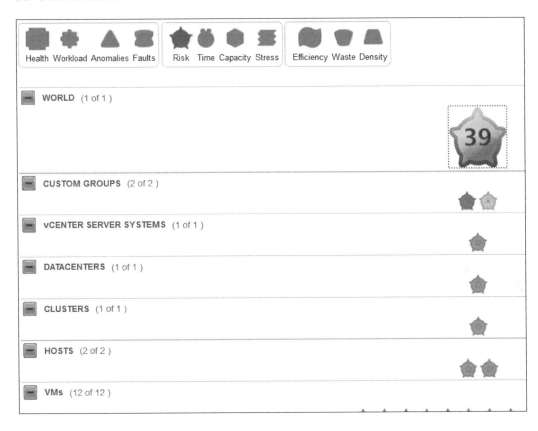

Our **Risk** score for the world object isn't great. Remember that the lower the score for **Risk** the better. The first thing that jumps out at us is all the orange skittles. Then we see that one of the datastores is actually red. If we click on it once, we'll see all the objects that are related to it. We should take note if the objects related to it are also having problems. If we double-click on the red datastore skittle, we'll see what the issues are.

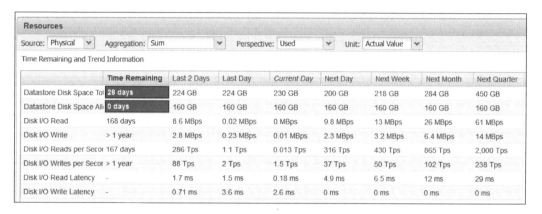

We can see that if we keep on with the current trends, we will run out of disk space in 28 days. Since it can take a while to procure storage, vC Ops is telling us that this is a critical alert, and we need to go ahead and get more storage. We can also alleviate this using Storage vMotion to move some of our VMs to other datastores.

Let's go back to our **Environment** tab and click on the **Risk** badge again. We see that one of our orange skittles represents the host cluster. If we had several clusters in vC Ops, we could click on the cluster to see the related objects highlighted. Now we'll go ahead and double-click on the cluster, and we will see the following screenshot:

We see we're getting critical alerts because our **Host Memory** has 0 days remaining. We need to either add more memory or check to see if we have any reclaimable waste. Also, our host CPU only has 70 days left, so it might actually be time to add another host.

Future risks don't always mean that we're just running out of capacity. It could just mean that we're seeing objects that are stressed. If we go back to our **Environment** tab and click on the **Stress** badge, it looks like we only have one stressed object, which is SQL VM.

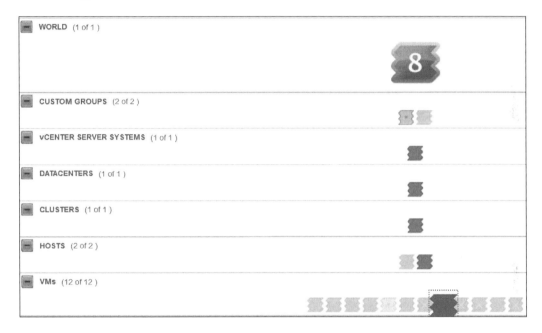

I've selected the VM, and it's showing us which other objects are related. Mostly it's green, so it looks like it's only the VM that's being stressed. If we double-click on the VM, we're taken to the **Planning** tab again. We can then click on the **Events** subtab to see how long it's been stressed and which events are causing it to be stressed.

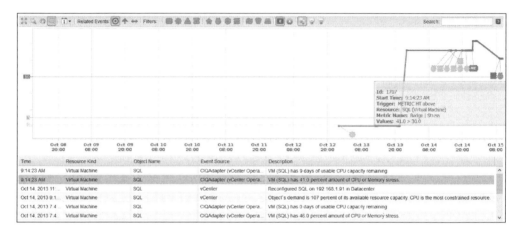

# Summary

In this chapter, we saw how to unlock some of the potential of vCenter Operations Manager. We started with taking a broad view of our environment, looking at some of the maintenance tasks administrators can perform to keep their environments running like well-oiled machines. We did this by looking at the Dashboard tab and then drilling into the major and minor badges that basically aren't green right now.

We then went for a more narrowed approach of looking at things. We knew where our problems existed, and we started there. If a VM was running slowly, we selected that VM, started broad, and homed in on issues. We did the same for datastore and networking issues. We could also do this for entire applications, sites, and so on, by putting VMs into groups.

Finally, we saw how to find potential future issues due to increased stress or lack of compute resources and storage space. This brings us seamlessly into our next chapter, which will be all about capacity management. We'll find out how we can optimize our environments, create what-if scenarios, and understand what kind of resources we need.

# 5
# Capacity Planning with vCenter Operations Manager

When most people think of vCenter Operations Manager, they only think about troubleshooting. However, there's a huge advantage to using vC Ops in comparison to other capacity planning software. Whenever I show someone vC Ops for the first time, they usually want it for troubleshooting, but they're able to justify buying it because of the capacity planning capabilities.

In this chapter, we'll cover:

- Optimizing our environment
- What-if scenarios
- The capacity analysis page

## Optimizing our environment

There are several options available to help us optimize our virtual environment within vCenter Operations Manager. In this section, we'll take a look at oversized and undersized VMs that will help our applications run better without wasting resources. We'll also see how powered-off VMs can waste space within our storage array or local storage. We'll then look at common VM configurations that can help us point out if we're using larger VMs than necessary by default. Similar to finding undersized VMs, we'll see how to identify hosts and clusters that are underused. And finally, we'll go through the broader topic of datastore waste in general.

# Undersized and oversized VMs

Optimization is a smaller function of capacity planning, but it can help us save resources within our environment, thereby possibly saving money! We do this by finding oversized and undersized VMs. An oversized VM is a virtual machine that has been assigned too many resources (CPU, memory, and so on) for the amount of load it has on average. For instance, if we have a VM with two vCPUs but it's using less than one, this VM is oversized. An undersized VM is the opposite, for example, we only have 2 GB of memory assigned to a VM but the application installed on it requires 8 GB. Some software vendors will specify larger hardware requirements than necessary. The hardware requirements should be driven by workload.

We can find these VMs by clicking on the **Planning** tab in our vC Ops UI and then clicking on the **Views** subtab. If we have **All Views** highlighted, we can scroll down to see **Oversized Virtual Machines** and **Undersized Virtual Machines** in the **Views Gallery**. These can also be found in the **Waste** category.

If we start with **Oversized Virtual Machines**, we'll see a list of VMs that have more resources than necessary, as shown in the following screenshot:

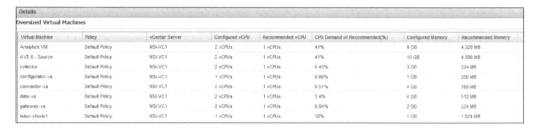

Let's take a look at our **Analytics VM**. We see that it is assigned the **Default Policy**. It's assigned to the **NSI-VC1** vCenter Server. Then we get to the important information. It has **2 vCPUs** under **Configured vCPU**. That means when this VM was created, the administrator gave it two vCPUs. This may have been recommended by the application owner or in the requirements for the server itself. Whatever the case, on average, it uses only 41 percent of the recommended vCPUs, as shown under **CPU Demand of Recommended(%)**. This means that the VM is actually only using 41 percent of one vCPU because **Recommended vCPU** is only **1 vCPU**. So even if we knock that VM down to one vCPU, it will still be at 41 percent CPU utilization. If we take a look at **Configured Memory**, we see **9 GB** and under **Recommended Memory**, it shows **4,320 MB**. It is safe to investigate the disparity and potentially reduce the amount of provisioned memory.

With that VM only, we gained back one vCPU and 4.5 GB of memory. Imagine if we have 50, 100, or 1000 VMs on this list. We might be able to hold off buying all that RAM we thought we needed or that extra physical host for a little while longer. There is no straightforward method of gaining this level of insight within vCenter. We can check CPU utilization for a certain time period, as well as memory utilization, but with vC Ops, we get the exact numbers we're using on average and what we could possibly give up.

Now, let's look at the **Undersized Virtual Machines** from the **Views Gallery**. Again, these are machines that haven't been given enough resources for what they're running on average. There are often very few VMs on this list just because most people have a tendency to over-allocate either due to pre-requisites or because we assign hardware the same way we do in physical environments, where we follow a vendor's requirements and rely on hardware over-allocation to handle scaling up a workload.

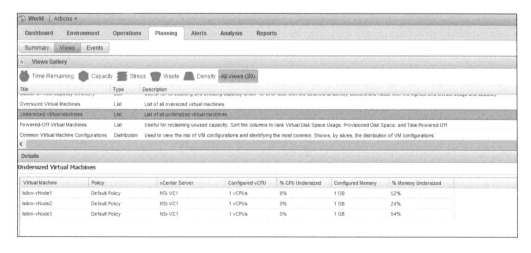

We see the same kind of information: **Virtual Machine**, **Policy**, and **vCenter Server**.

Then we see our **Configured vCPU** and **% CPU Undersized**. For the **Isilon-vNode1** VM, it says we have **1 vCPUs**, which is **0%** undersized. This just means that vCPU is not undersized for this VM; we can leave it as is. If we look at the **Configured Memory** and **% Memory Undersized**, we see that it has **1 GB** of memory assigned to it by the administrator that created the VM and it should have **52%** more assigned to it, meaning it should have a little over 1.5 GB. Finding undersized VMs doesn't exactly lend itself to saving on hardware, but our VMs, and thereby our applications, are in comparison to run better with the recommended resources.

# Powered-off VMs

There's another view in the **Views Gallery** that's worth checking out. The **Powered-Off Virtual Machines** view shows us VMs that have been powered off and what percentage of time they've been powered off. We might have several of these in our environment because they were used for testing or they've been replaced by newer servers, or perhaps a developer asked for it and used it for a few months and now they've moved on to something else.

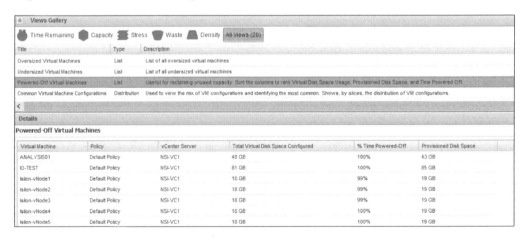

Again, we see the **Virtual Machine**, **Policy** and **vCenter Server** columns by which it's managed. We then see the **Total Virtual Disk Space Configured** and the **Provisioned Disk Space** columns. Remember that VMs that are powered off do not take CPU, memory, or network resources. However, they do still take up space. As we can see from the % **Time Powered-Off** column, we have several VMs that have been powered off for 99 percent or 100 percent of the time since they were created. If we were to get rid of those VMs and reclaim that space, we could get several hundred gigabytes of storage back for new VMs. Therefore, we don't need to purchase more disks, shelves for the storage array, or even entire arrays, depending on how large our environment is. We should also take note that we can assign different policies to different objects and we can sort by policy as shown in the previous table. This would be useful if we have a lot of templates. It would be worth creating a new policy for them so we can avoid getting a *false positive* on the tables such as **Powered-Off Virtual Machines**.

# More optimization options

If we click on the **Planning** tab and then on the **Views** subtab, we can find more optimization options. Here, we'll click on the **Waste** category to see all of our optimization options, which are as follows:

- **Oversized Virtual Machines**
- **Undersized Virtual Machines**
- **Powered-Off Virtual Machines**
- **Common Virtual Machine Configurations**
- **Underused Hosts and Clusters**
- **Datastore Waste**

# Common virtual machine configurations

If we click on **Common Virtual Machine Configurations**, we see the following pie chart:

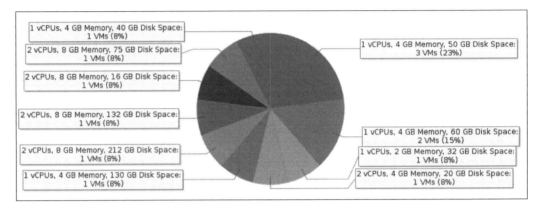

Here we see what our most common VMs look like. It's very likely that at one point or another, a template was created to deploy VMs quickly. If we see a large amount of our pie chart containing four vCPUs or 8 GB of RAM, we might have a template out there that is larger than necessary for our average servers. In that case, we might not only want to look at our oversized VMs but also go out and correct the template to use less resources by default. We can always resize the VMs that need to be larger.

# Underused hosts and clusters

Now we'll click on the **Underused Hosts and Clusters** view. This looks a lot like our **Undersized Virtual Machines** view, except it's for the entire cluster. It shows us the cluster it's talking about and then tells us the recommended resources.

In the previous screenshot, I've shown only the recommendations. As we can see, it shows I have **8 CPUs** under the **CPU Count** column, but I only need **3 CPUs** for the VMs I'm running. As for **Memory Capacity**, I have **27 GB**, but I only need **10 GB**. Also, I have **1.7 TB** of disk space, but I only need **345 GB**. I'm not suggesting that we start tearing out the hardware, but it's good to know there are still enough resources on this cluster for more VMs. We could also use these extra hosts in another cluster, if we have more in our environment, to help reduce the strain on other existing clusters.

# Datastore waste

The **Datastore Waste** view gives us some of the same information that the **Powered-Off Virtual Machines** view gives us along with some other useful data.

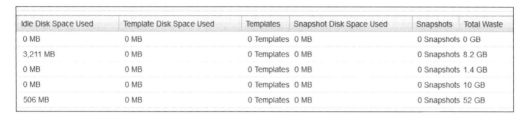

The left-hand side of the table, shown in the previous screenshot, is mostly informational. It shows us which **Datastore** we're looking at, including local datastores, as well as the disk space used for each one. To the very right, it tells us how much space is used by powered-off VMs. The right-hand side of the table is a little more interesting as shown in the following screenshot:

| Idle Disk Space Used | Template Disk Space Used | Templates | Snapshot Disk Space Used | Snapshots | Total Waste |
|---|---|---|---|---|---|
| 0 MB | 0 MB | 0 Templates | 0 MB | 0 Snapshots | 0 GB |
| 3,211 MB | 0 MB | 0 Templates | 0 MB | 0 Snapshots | 8.2 GB |
| 0 MB | 0 MB | 0 Templates | 0 MB | 0 Snapshots | 1.4 GB |
| 0 MB | 0 MB | 0 Templates | 0 MB | 0 Snapshots | 10 GB |
| 506 MB | 0 MB | 0 Templates | 0 MB | 0 Snapshots | 52 GB |

We can see the **Idle Disk Space Used** column, which again goes back to whether we're really using the VMs these disks are attached to. We can also see how much space our templates are taking up. We sometimes forget about old templates because they're no longer in the vCenter inventory, but are still taking up room on a datastore, or because we don't go to the **VMs and Folders** view on vCenter.

The next column shows us how much space our snapshots are taking up. This is very important! Snapshots grow larger as time goes by and more changes are made to that VM. They are not meant to be used as backups. It's okay to leave them for a week or so, but any longer should be concerning. If we see that a large or even moderate part of our storage is being used by snapshots, it's time to go through our VMs and delete some of them. Finally, the last column, **Total Waste**, gives us the totals from the rest of the columns.

If we're looking for an easy way to find snapshots, we can use a tool called RVTools found at http://www.robware.net/. When we run RVTools in our environment, it shows us a point-in-time snapshot of our virtual infrastructure. There is currently a vSnapshot tab we can look at to find the snapshots that are in our environment, including snapshots we may not necessarily see via vCenter. Please note that RVTools is not a VMware product. It was created by Rob de Veij and is updated by him. See the About section on the website to find out more (http://www.robware. net/index.php/about).

Snapshots are basically point-in-time states that can be saved in our virtual machine. Much like Windows uses Restore Points, we can take a snapshot of a VM before an upgrade or applying patches. If the upgrade doesn't go well or there's a bug in the patches, we can easily revert back to our snapshot by right-clicking on the VM. We can create several snapshots for one VM, each representing a different point in time. According to the VMware KB article ((1015180) http://kb.vmware.com/selfservice/ microsites/search.do?language=en_US&cmd=displayKC&ex ternalId=1015180), "If a virtual machine is running off a snapshot, it is making changes to a child or sparse disk. The more write operations made to this disk, the larger it grows." If a snapshot were to fill up an entire datastore, depending on which vSphere version we're running, our VMs sharing that datastore will either pause or be automatically powered down. The only way to recover from this is to delete the snapshot or Storage vMotion and other VMs off that datastore to free up storage space. This can take a very long time on a full datastore. For more information on snapshots, please see the following VMware KB article: http://kb.vmware.com/selfservice/microsites/search. do?language=en_US&cmd=displayKC&externalId=1025279.

# What-if scenarios

vCenter Operations Manager has the ability to create what-if scenarios, which allow us to get an idea of how our environment would handle it if we added or removed VMs or hardware. It tells us if we have enough compute resources and space and gives us a report on the results. To get to these what-if scenarios, we go to the **Planning** tab again and click on the **Summary** subtab.

The **New what-if scenario** option is only available if we've selected the cluster object or host objects in the tree on the left. With other objects, the option will appear to be grayed out. After we click on the **New what-if scenario** link, we are taken to the **What-if scenarios** wizard. The first screen is the **Views** screen as shown in the following screenshot. There are three views shown and they relate to the three views from the **Planning** tab, under the **Time Remaining** view, in the **Views Gallery** on the **Views** subtab.

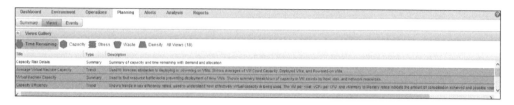

If we were to click on the **Views** tab from the beginning, click on one of the views and select **Create a new what-if scenario**. We wouldn't be presented with the views first. It would take us directly to the **Change Type** screen. We only get the **View** screen if we're on the **Planning** tab, under the **Summary** subtab and we've selected one of the correlating **Time Remaining** views from the **View Gallery**.

The first **View** is **Average Virtual Machine Capacity - Trend**. So this option will find obstacles based on the average VM count capacity, deployed VMs, and powered-on VMs trends.

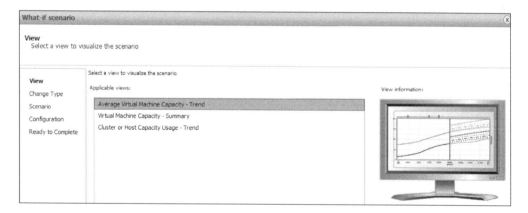

# Hardware changes

If we pick this view, the next screen gives us an option of whether we want to change the Hosts and Datastores or Virtual machines. If we change Hosts and Datastores, we're presented with the options to **Add Host**, **Remove Host**, or **Restore Host** as shown in the following screenshot:

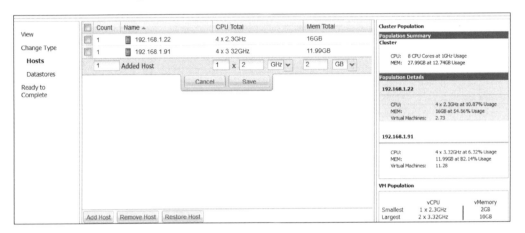

In the previous example, I've chosen **Add Host**. We can see my added host in the list. We can change the quantity, the **CPU Total**, and the **Mem Total**. This will not actually change anything within our environment. It only maps out what it would look like. On the right-hand side, we see the details of our environment. We see that there are **8 CPU Cores** and **27.99GB** of memory in the environment. It then breaks it down by each host, and finally, tells us the compute resources used by our smallest and largest VMs.

If we click on **Save** and then **Next**, we're taken to the **Datastores** screen. We have the same options here: **Add Datastore**, **Remove Datastore**, and **Restore Datastore**. We would use this screen if we were going to change the storage in our virtual environment and if we wanted to see how it would affect things. Perhaps we want to figure out how much storage it would take to alleviate some of our current storage woes. We can see exactly how much additional storage is needed to make things work more efficiently.

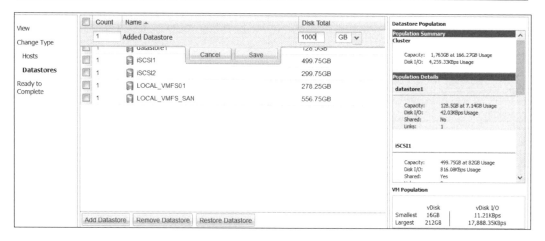

Again, on the right we're shown the details of our datastores for the entire cluster, which is then broken down by datastore. We're also shown the **vDisk** and **vDisk I/O** for the smallest VM and the largest VM. As with the hosts, I can add several datastores of the same size by changing the quantity or adding different-sized datastores. If we click on **Save** and **Next** here, we're taken to the **Ready to Complete** screen.

The **Ready to Complete** screen just shows us a summary of the things we've added within our **What-If Scenario**. The next part is a little counterintuitive if we don't realize right away that the views in the **What-If Scenario** correlate directly with the views in the **Views Gallery**. After we click on **Finish** on the **Ready to Complete** screen, we should be on the **Planning** tab under the **Views** subtab and on the view from the **View Gallery**, which we selected on the first screen of the **What-If Scenario** wizard.

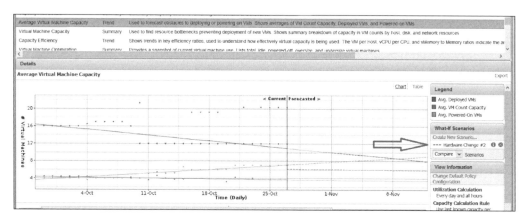

Keep in mind that there is no pop-up report after we create a new What-if scenario. We must navigate to the proper view under the **Planning** tab to find our scenarios. We can export them to create a report or deliverable, but this is a manual process.

As shown in the previous screenshot, we've selected the **Average Virtual Machine Capacity** view. On the right of the graph, in the **Details** pane, we have the **Legend** showing **Avg. Deployed VMs** in blue, **Avg. VM Count Capacity** in red, and **Avg. Powered-On VMs** in yellow. Below the **Legend**, we see our **What-if Scenarios**, where right now there's only one, called **Hardware Changes #2**. We can click on the information icon (the circle with an **i** on it) to see what this scenario is, or we can click on the **x** with a circle around it to delete the scenario completely. If we take a look at the graph, the vertical line shows us today's date. Anything before this date are the actual statistics and trends. Anything after that line is the forecast based on trends. The straight lines show us what the forecast is with our current hardware. The dashed lines show us what the trends would look like with our given what-if scenario. We can also click on the **Table** view to see this information in tabular format. This will give us three tables with specific numbers for the average deployed VMs, average VM count capacity, and average powered-on VMs.

By default, we compare what-if scenarios, but we can also combine them. We'd want to combine scenarios to see what kind of hardware is necessary if we're planning to add more VMs. For instance, let's say we're already pretty optimized and are using most of our hardware resources. However, we know we need to add 50 more VMs because the developers are creating a new product. We can create the what-if scenario with the 50 more VMs and see how our current environment would handle it. Then, we can create a new what-if scenario by adding more hardware to see how much would be necessary for the environment to continue running successfully. We can only see this if we combine the scenarios. Comparing the scenarios does not take the other scenario into account.

 When we're adding VMs using a what-if scenario, we want to keep in mind that vC Ops is still, by default, taking into account things such as HA and CPU contention.

So, if we create another what-if scenario as we did before, we can click on the pull-down menu on the right and select **Combine** instead. Let's say we don't want to add a datastore, but we want to add two hosts. By default, we'll see a graph showing both the scenarios. If we click on **Combine**, we'll see the following screenshot:

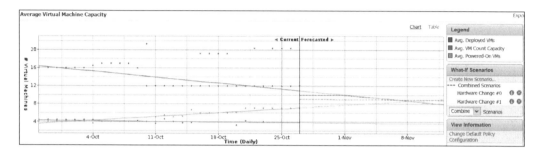

On the right-hand side, we see two hardware changes, **Hardware Changes #0** and **Hardware Changes #1**, but on top, we see **Combined Scenarios**. If we were to compare scenarios, the little lines to the left of the scenario would tell us which line pattern stood for each scenario. Since we've combined them, we see there's only one line pattern, a sort of dashed line that shows us what it would look like if we applied both scenarios to our environment.

Now, just because we selected the **Average Virtual Machine Capacity** view when we started our what-if scenario, doesn't mean we can't look at the other views for the scenarios we've already set up. If we click on the **Virtual Machine Capacity** view under the **Views** subtab, we're shown what is in the following screenshot:

| Capacity Remaining | | | |
|---|---|---|---|
| | Actual | Hardware Change #0 | Hardware Change #1 |
| Host CPU | 15 VMs | 12 VMs | 30 VMs |
| Host Memory | Over by 0.92 VMs | Over by 0.59 VMs | 4.3 VMs |
| Disk Space | 6 VMs | 7.6 VMs | 6 VMs |
| Disk I/O Read | 884 VMs | 884 VMs | 884 VMs |
| Disk I/O Write | 947 VMs | 947 VMs | 947 VMs |
| Disk I/O Reads per Second | 827 VMs | 827 VMs | 827 VMs |
| Disk I/O Writes per Second | 824 VMs | 824 VMs | 824 VMs |
| Network I/O Received Rate | 1,005 VMs | 1,005 VMs | 1,005 VMs |
| Network I/O Transmitted Rate | 997 VMs | 997 VMs | 997 VMs |
| **Summary** | **Over by 0.92 VMs** | **Over by 0.59 VMs** | **4.3 VMs** |

This table, as well as the following ones, show a comparison of the two scenarios I've created (**Hardware Change #0** added one host and a datastore and **Hardware Change #1** added two hosts). The first table shows **Capacity Remaining**. The best example of the results shown by the what-if scenarios is next to **Host Memory**. As shown in the **Actual** column, we now are using more memory than we have. We're over by **0.92 VMs**. Using additional hardware, as suggested by **Hardware Change #0**, we're still over by 0.59 VMs. However, if we were to use only **Hardware Change #1**, we actually have enough memory for 4.3 more VMs. Again, this is not combining the scenarios, rather it shows us what each one would do individually. We can combine them and obviously we'd have even more capacity remaining.

The next table we're shown is for **Time Remaining**. This gives us information similar to that of **Capacity Remaining**, but it's broken down by how many days we have left before we run out.

| Time Remaining | | | |
|---|---|---|---|
| | Actual | Hardware Change #0 | Hardware Change #1 |
| Host CPU | 101 days | 121 days | 258 days |
| Host Memory | **0 days** | **0 days** | **13 days** |
| Disk Space | 350 days | > 1 year | 350 days |
| Disk I/O Read | > 1 year | > 1 year | > 1 year |
| Disk I/O Write | > 1 year | > 1 year | > 1 year |
| Disk I/O Reads per Second | > 1 year | > 1 year | > 1 year |
| Disk I/O Writes per Second | > 1 year | > 1 year | > 1 year |
| Network I/O Received Rate | > 1 year | > 1 year | > 1 year |
| Network I/O Transmitted Rate | > 1 year | > 1 year | > 1 year |
| **Summary** | **0 days** | **0 days** | **13 days** |

As expected, we see the most constraints around **Host Memory**. With our **Actual** hardware and the hardware added in **Hardware Change #0**, we have **0 days** left. With **Hardware Change #1**, we have **13 days** left.

Other tables shown are as follows:

- **VM Capacity**
- **Deployed**
- **Powered On**
- **Capacity**
- **Usage**
- **Host Usage**

- **Effective Demand**
- **Reserved Capacity**
- **Overcommitted Allocation**
- **Host Overcommitted Allocation**

| Host Overcommited Allocation | Actual | Hardware Change #0 | Hardware Change #1 |
|---|---|---|---|
| Host CPU | 26% | 23% | 13% |
| Host Memory | **120%** | **112%** | **56%** |
| Disk Space | 52% | 49% | 52% |
| Disk I/O Read | - | - | - |
| Disk I/O Write | - | - | - |
| Disk I/O Reads per Second | - | - | - |
| Disk I/O Writes per Second | - | - | - |
| Network I/O Received Rate | - | - | - |
| Network I/O Transmitted Rate | - | - | - |
| **Summary** | **120%** | **112%** | **56%** |

The **Host Overcommitted Allocation** table shows us the percentage by which our hosts are over-allocated. The **Host Memory** is still the constraint; as we see with our current hardware, we're over-allocated by **120%**. Obviously, adding more hardware makes that percentage lower as seen in the tables. The summary shows us the most constrained resource.

Finally, let's click on our last view, **Cluster or Host Capacity Usage**. We're shown more trends and forecasts, but it shows a little more in-depth information about some of the hardware. The following screenshot shows information for **CPU** and **Memory**.

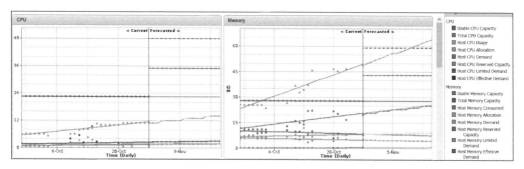

We're also shown Disk I/O information in the following screenshot:

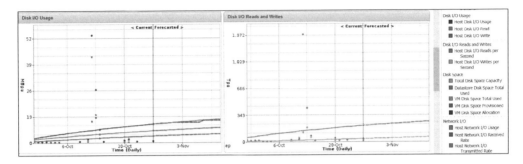

Finally, we're also **Disk Space** and **Network I/O** in the following screenshot:

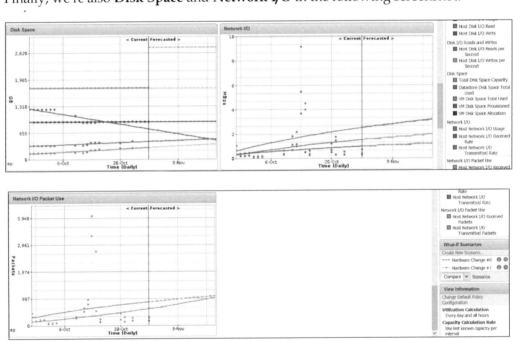

Again, these graphs show us the current environment on the left of the vertical line and the forecasted environment to the right of the vertical line.

I'd like to make one last note about adding hardware using a what-if scenario. We don't have to add an entire host if we're looking to just add memory. If we create a new what-if scenario, select **Hosts & Datastores** in the **Change Type** screen, we will then be taken to the **Hosts** screen as shown in the following screenshot. If we click on one of our existing hosts, we can change the **CPU Total** and the **Mem Total** columns by entering the new totals and then clicking on **Save**. Note that the quantity is grayed out here though.

> If we want to add more memory to a host, we need to ensure that we have open RAM slots and that we're following vendor best practices when adding more. There is also the option of replacing the current DIMMs with DIMMs that have more memory per stick. If these options do not work, we will need to add more physical hosts.

# Virtual machine changes

Let's look at a different kind of what-if scenario where instead of adding hardware, we see what it looks like if we wanted to add **Virtual Machines**. Again, we'll click on **New What-if Scenario** and select a view if necessary. However, in the **Change Type** screen, we'll select **Virtual machines** as shown in the following screenshot:

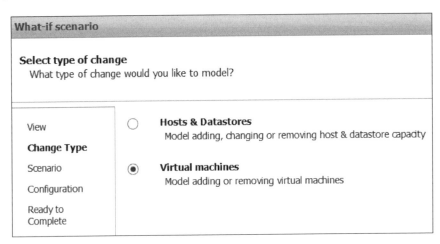

Using the **Virtual machines Change Type**, we're presented with three scenarios instead of the **Hosts & Datastores** screen.

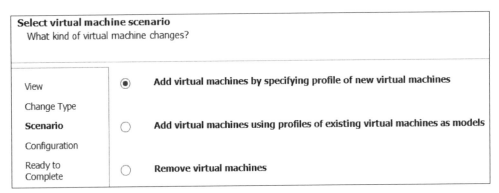

The first scenario, **Add virtual machines by specifying profile of new virtual machines**, allows us to add virtual machines manually. When we select the first scenario and click on **Next**, we're shown the following **Configuration** screen:

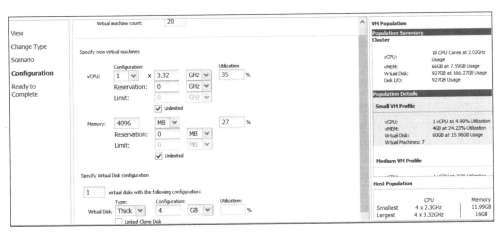

At the top of the **Configuration** screen, we can specify how many VMs we'd like to add. For instance, if our developers have requested 20 VMs of a certain size, we would put 20 next to the **Virtual machine count** field. We can then specify how many vCPUs we want to use. We're given default utilization numbers based on what vC Ops has learned. If we have an idea that the utilization will be higher because these VMs are going to be highly utilized, we can go ahead and change that number. We can also specify how much memory we'd like to assign and again, either accept the default or enter in our own number. For both **vCPU** and **Memory**, we can attach reservations and limits. At the bottom of the **Configuration** screen, we can also specify the disk information. We can say whether we'd like it to be **Thin** or **Thick** provisioned, how big it should be, and even whether we'd like it to be a linked clone. After we've specified all this information, click on **Next** and then go to the **Ready to Complete** screen, which again gives us a summary of the information we've input.

Now, we can go through and click on our different views as we did when we made the hardware changes. Instead of seeing the scenarios called **Hardware Change**, they're named after how many VMs we've added. The following example shows what it looks like when we click on the information icon next to the scenario:

| Scenario: Add 20 New VMs | | | |
| --- | --- | --- | --- |

**Add VM Profile**

Adding **20** of the following new profile:

| **CPU** | **CPU Utilization** | **Memory Capacity** | **Memory Utilization** |
| --- | --- | --- | --- |
| 1 x 3 GHz | 35% | 4 GB | 27% |
| **CPU Reservation** | **CPU Limit** | **Memory Reservation** | **Memory Limit** |
| 0 GHz | Unlimited | 0 GB | Unlimited |
| **Disk Provisioned** | **Disk Used** | **Virtual Disk Type** | **Linked-Clone Disk** |
| 4 GB | 0% | Thick provisioned | False |

Now, we can go through each of the views as we did before with the hardware changes. In this case, it shows us what happens to our current hardware if we add 20 VMs. As an example, if we click on the **Views** tab and then on the **Virtual Machine Capacity** view (as shown in the following screenshot), we can see right now we're currently over-allocated on memory by 0.95 VMs. If we were to add 20 VMs, we would be over by 19 VMs. We might be curious about why we're not over by 21 (or 20.95) VMs in this scenario. Keep in mind that we specified things such as CPU and memory utilization, which allows vSphere to do some over-allocating and so on. Given the scenario I put forth, this is vC Ops' best guess on what our utilization will be and by how many VMs we are over.

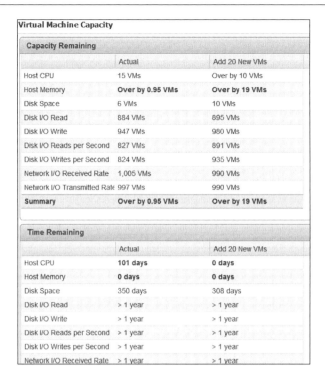

I won't go through every view again as it gives similar information to that covered for the hardware changes. Let's take a look at the next scenario: We choose **Virtual Machine Change Type** in the **What-if Scenario** wizard and **Add virtual machines using profiles of existing virtual machines as models**. With this scenario, we're able to use the current VM profiles to model what any new VMs might look like. This will make more sense if we look at the following screenshot:

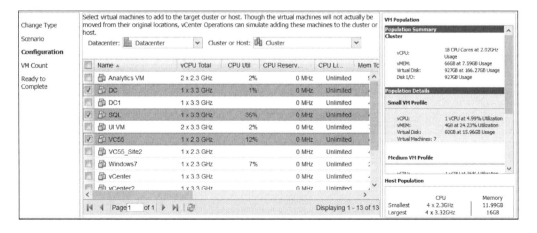

It shows us a pull-down menu so that we can select from which **Datacenter** we'd like to choose VMs as well as from which **Cluster or Host** we'd like to choose VMs. Once we've specified those things, we'll see our VMs populate the list. We might use this scenario if we add the same types of VMs over and over, such as the same type of application servers and database servers. Next we will put a check by the two VMs that represent these types of servers. Then we click on **Next** and specify the amount of each server that we would like, as shown in the following screenshot:

| VM Count | Name ▲ | vCPU Total | CPU Util | Mem Total | Mem Util | Dis |
|---|---|---|---|---|---|---|
| Review the list of machines selected. Increase the multiplier to create more than one of any machine. | | | | | | |
| 1 | DC | 1 x 3.3 GHz | 1% | 4096 MB | 19% | |
| 1 | SQL | 1 x 3.3 GHz | 36% | 4096 MB | 28% | 1 |
| 1 | VC55 | 1 x 2.3 GHz | 12% | 4096 MB | 41% | |

We may have 25 application servers that we'd like to add but only five database servers. vC Ops makes it real easy to change the VM count in the **VM Count** screen of the wizard. Now, click on **Next** and we will be taken to the familiar **Ready to Complete** screen to get our summary, then click on **Finish**. We can again browse through the different views to see how adding our 25 application server VMs and five database server VMs will work in our environment.

The last **Virtual Machine Change Type** scenario is **Remove virtual machines**. This is pretty self-explanatory. Essentially, we can remove VMs and see how many compute resources and storage we will gain back. Much like the second scenario, we will see a list of our VMs. If we'd like to model what it would be like to remove them, we simply check the boxes next to that VM or several VMs. Then click on **Next** and **Finish** and browse the various views to see the results.

# Hardware changes and virtual machine changes

It's all well and good to see how we can rightsize our current environment. What if we're planning a lot of growth in the future and need to figure out exactly what kind of hardware we need for a particular amount of new VMs? Here, we can use the **Combined** option as well.

As an example, let's say we're going to add 100 VMs with 2 vCPUs and 8 GB of memory, and they each have 80 GB of disk space. We'll create our **What-if Scenario** using the **Virtual Machine Change Type** option using these specifications. With the current hardware in my lab, we're shown the following screenshot for **Capacity Remaining** in our **Virtual Machine Capacity** view:

| Virtual Machine Capacity | | |
| --- | --- | --- |
| **Capacity Remaining** | | |
| | Actual | Add 100 New VMs |
| Host CPU | 15 VMs | Over by 98 VMs |
| Host Memory | **Over by 0.95 VMs** | **Over by 101 VMs** |
| Disk Space | 6 VMs | Over by 97 VMs |
| Disk I/O Read | 884 VMs | 869 VMs |
| Disk I/O Write | 947 VMs | 910 VMs |
| Disk I/O Reads per Second | 827 VMs | 854 VMs |
| Disk I/O Writes per Second | 824 VMs | 897 VMs |
| Network I/O Received Rate | 1,005 VMs | 910 VMs |
| Network I/O Transmitted Rate | 997 VMs | 910 VMs |
| **Summary** | **Over by 0.95 VMs** | **Over by 101 VMs** |

We see with our current hardware that we have enough room for 15 VMs. When it comes to **Host CPU**, we're still over 0.95 VMs from a **Host Memory** perspective and we have room for VMs from a storage perspective. If we were to add our 100 VMs, we would be over by around 100 VMs for all of these categories.

Now we'll create a new **What-if Scenario** to add hardware to our environment. See the following screenshot for a summary of the hardware that has been added:

**What-if scenario configuration**

**Host Configurations:**

| Change Type | Multiplier | Profile name | CPU | Memory |
|---|---|---|---|---|
| Adding | 5 | Added Host | 4 x 2GHz | 100GB |
| Changing | 1 | 192.168.1.91 | 4 x 3.32GHz | 100GB |
| Changing | 1 | 192.168.1.22 | 4 x 2.3GHz | 100GB |

**Datastore Configurations:**

| Change Type | Multiplier | Profile name | Size |
|---|---|---|---|
| Adding | 10 | Added Datastore | 1,000GB |

Now we have both of our scenarios created. If we click on the pull-down menu to **Combine** them, we're shown the following information for **Virtual Machine Capacity**:

**Virtual Machine Capacity**

**Capacity Remaining**

| | Actual | Combined |
|---|---|---|
| Host CPU | **15 VMs** | **Over by 85 VMs** |
| Host Memory | **Over by 0.95 VMs** | **Over by 16 VMs** |
| Disk Space | 6 VMs | 30 VMs |
| Disk I/O Read | 884 VMs | 869 VMs |
| Disk I/O Write | 947 VMs | 910 VMs |
| Disk I/O Reads per Second | 827 VMs | 854 VMs |
| Disk I/O Writes per Second | 824 VMs | 897 VMs |
| Network I/O Received Rate | 1,005 VMs | 910 VMs |
| Network I/O Transmitted Rate | 997 VMs | 910 VMs |
| **Summary** | **Over by 0.95 VMs** | **Over by 85 VMs** |

As we can see, I've not added nearly enough hardware to cover what we need for all 100 VMs, but I've got an idea now. I'm still over by 85 VMs when it comes to CPU because I didn't change the CPU on any of my existing hosts that don't have much and I kept the **Host CPU** the same for the new servers I added. I'm getting a little closer with **Host Memory** as I'm only over by 16 VMs. I'm doing pretty well on **Disk Space** though, even after I added 100 VMs, I still have room for 30 more. That's because I added 10 1 TB datastores in my **What-if Scenario**. Now I can go back and add more CPU and memory to see exactly what I'll need to add my 100 VMs.

Workflow for a What-if scenario:

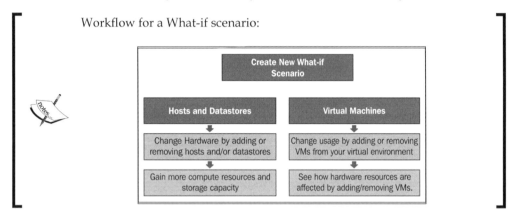

# The capacity analysis page

On the vC Ops custom dashboard, found at `https://<UI_VM_IP_Address>/vcops-custom/`, there is a **Forensics** tab as shown in the following screenshot. If we hover over the **Forensics** tab and click on **Capacity Analysis**, we're taken to the **CAPACITY ANALYSIS** page.

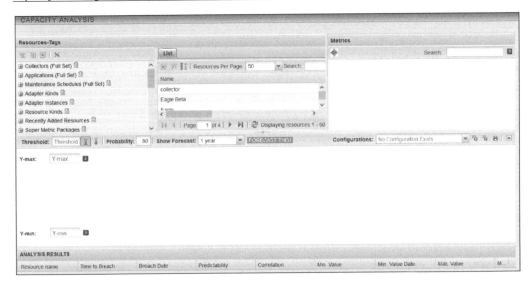

 This page is only available with the Enterprise version of vCenter Operations Manager.

As shown, the **CAPACITY ANALYSIS** page has two widgets on the top, consisting of **Resource-Tags** and **Metrics**. At the bottom of the page, we can see a graph of a forecast for a chosen metric. The **Resource-Tags** widget contains all of the resources in our environment. Some of these have been tagged by default as certain kinds of resources and some are manually tagged by the administrator. To the right is the **Metrics** widget, which is not populated by default. It only populates with relative metrics after we've chosen a resource-tag and entity from the **List**. One thing to watch out for is that once we've selected a resource-tag, we cannot select a different resource-tag if we change our mind. Our list may then appear to be empty. We actually need to click on the deselect all icon to choose another resource-tag. If the two resources we selected have entities in common, then those will show up in the **List**. If we are looking for a particular resource, we may type it in the search field as well.

Let's try a couple of examples to get the hang of it. If we click on the **Abnormal** resource-tag under **Health Ranges**, we're presented with a list of entities that have been tagged as abnormal. If we select something from the **List**, we are shown the metrics that we can graph out on the **Metrics** widget. We then need to double-click one of these metrics for it to show up in the graph below. I've chosen to show **Average Host Workload (%)** in the following screenshot:

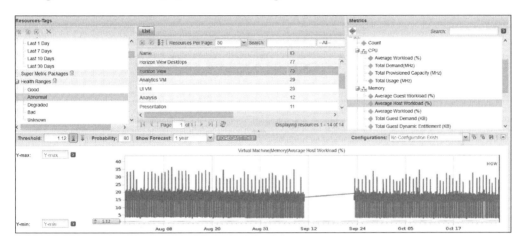

This is another case where vC Ops is a tad confusing. The previous graph tells us what the use looks like for memory (**Average Host Workload (%)**). The Y axis shows us the percentage of memory, which looks to fluctuate between 5 percent and around 35 percent. The X axis shows us the date that goes from the beginning of August to the end of October. To the left of the graph, we can set our maximum percentage and minimum percentage by entering numbers next to the **Y-max** and the **Y-min** fields and then clicking on the blue arrow next to it. We can't really click on the graph or zoom in as we can with other graphs within vC Ops. The only way to manipulate it is to change the maximum and minimum values.

Right above the graph is the **FORECAST THIS!** bar. On the left is the **Threshold** value. We can enter a value here or actually change the threshold bar on the graph, which appears in orange in the previous screenshot. Clicking-and-dragging it up or down will set the threshold. The arrows next to the **Threshold** field specify whether we're setting a maximum threshold (the up arrow) or a minimum threshold (the down arrow). For example, if I wanted to be warned when my **Average Host Workload** kept going above 40 percent, I would set my threshold value to 40. The next value in the bar is **Probability**. This number reflects the percentage of time this metric is above my threshold (or below if we set a minimum threshold). We'll leave it at 80 for this example. Next, we see the **Show Forecast** field. There are five values we can set this to: To Breach Date, 3 months, 6 months, 9 months, or 1 year. We'll leave it at a year for this example. Now we can click on the **FORECAST THIS!** button to see the **ANALYSIS RESULTS**, which are presented below the graph and shown in the following screenshot:

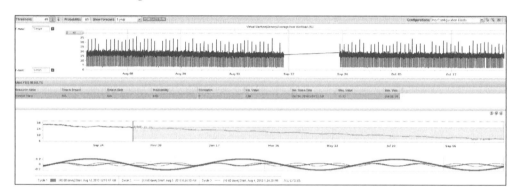

In the table right below the **ANALYSIS RESULTS** heading, we see the following columns:

- **Resource name**: This is the name of the resource we've selected above.

- **Time to Breach**: This is the amount of time until the metric values have crossed the threshold time taking into consideration **Probability**.

- **Breach Date**: This is the actual date of the predicted breach.

- **Predictability**: This is a value between 0 and 1. The closer the value is to 1, the higher the rate of predictability and therefore, the higher the chance the breach date is correct.

- **Correlation**: vC Ops can find whether this value correlates to other metrics. If it does, we can click on that value and a window will pop up with information about the other metrics.

- **Min. Value**: This value is predicted and is the minimum value that we are most likely to see from our metric during our forecast period.

- **Min. Value Date**: This is the date on which our **Min. Value** occurs.

- **Max. Value**: This value is also predicted and is the maximum value that we are most likely to see from our metric during our forecast period.

- **Max. Value Date**: This is the date on which our **Max. Value** occurs.

- Below the table, we see two more graphs. The top graph shows us previous and forecasted behaviour. Again, there is a vertical line separating the past from the future. The solid blue line going through the graph is the predicted value for the metric at the given time, with percentage on the Y axis and the date on the X axis. We see the orange values representing our **Max** and **Min** and the shaded area represents the predictability bounds.

According to the vCenter Operations Manager Enterprise Users Guide, the bottom graph is "a graph showing the calculated cycles in the metric's behaviour." If we click on the **ALL CYCLES** link below the graph, we can see a table of the cycles as well as their **Relative Power**. The cycles are representative of a pattern that correlates to a period of time. These patterns are used to help forecast future performance.

| Cycle | Cycle Start Time | Relative Power | |
|---|---|---|---|
| [40.00 days] | Aug 12, 2013 12:53:47 AM | 1 | Re |
| [13.00 days] | Aug 5, 2013 8:24:13 AM | 0.09 | |
| [10.00 days] | Aug 4, 2013 1:24:20 PM | 0.08 | |

One last thing to note about the **CAPACITY ANALYSIS** page is that we can save our configurations for later use. If we click on the save configuration icon next to **Configuration**, we can easily go back to this configuration at a later date.

# Summary

Capacity planning is an integral part of vCenter Operations Manager. I would say it's as important, if not more important than the troubleshooting aspects of it. Capacity planning can be used to optimize our virtual infrastructure and save money on our budget when done correctly. Utilizing vC Ops to do our capacity planning can also save us time by reducing manual calculations.

Capacity planning can mean a few things. The first thing we went over is optimizing our environment by checking for undersized and oversized VMs. If we have undersized VMs, we're using more of our computer's resources than necessary and essentially losing money. If we have oversized VMs, our applications are likely to be running slower than they should because they don't have the necessary resources to keep them running the way they should. There are also other views under the planning tab that can give us an idea of what our entire environment looks like and the kind of waste we might have. Remember to beware of snapshots! We can use vC Ops to tell us right away how we're wasting resources, if we are.

We can also plan for larger growth using vC Ops and what-if scenarios. These what-if scenarios allow us to model what our environment would look like if we were to add/remove hardware resources or add/remove VMs. Essentially, it comes down to adding supply or adding demand and finding the right balance between them. We can compare what-if scenarios as well as combine them to predict growth.

In the next chapter, we'll go over the reports tab and how we use reports to collect information, as well as schedule reports to be sent as notifications. We will also go over creating custom reports. These reports really come in handy as a weekly catch-up or something to send to the management team to give them an idea of what's going on in the environment.

# 6
# Reports

Another great thing about vCenter Operations Manager is the reporting functionality. The previous chapters were all about going through the dashboards and finding issues or capacity planning while we're actually in the **user interface (UI)**. However, we can create reports and even schedule them to run on a routine basis to get a quick glance of our environment. In this chapter, we'll go through how to create and use these reports for ourselves or even send them to other people within the IT department.

The topics that we'll cover in this chapter are as follows:

- Built-in and customized reports
- Custom reports
- Analysis of built-in reports

# Built-in reports

vC Ops has an extensive list of built-in reports we can run. We can find the reports under the **Reports** tab shown as follows:

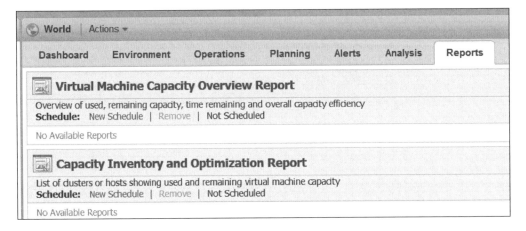

The following reports are included under the **Reports** tab:

- **Virtual Machine Capacity Overview Report**
- **Capacity Inventory and Optimization Report**
- **Virtual Machine Optimization Report**
- **Idle Virtual Machines Report**
- **Oversized Virtual Machines Report**
- **Undersized Virtual Machines Report**
- **Powered Off Virtual Machines Report**
- **Host Utilization Report**
- **Configured Host Capacity Report**
- **Cluster or Host Capacity Inventory Report**
- **Virtual Machine List Report**
- **VM Average and Peak Storage Access Latency Report**
- **Cluster/Host Utilization Report**
- **Average/Peak Datastore Latency and Throughput Report**
- **Health Score and Alert Trend Report**

As we can see, we have about 15 reports ready to be run at any time. Each report has a **Run Now** button next to it. As shown in the following screenshot, when we click on **Run Now**, it shows us the date when it was **Created**, **Run time**, **Status**, and the type of Download that we'd like to have. When the report is finished processing, the status will be listed as **Completed** with the current date, and we can either select a **PDF** or **CSV** type of download depending on whether we'll view it in Adobe or Excel:

This allows us to run a report any time we want. However, we can also schedule a report to run routinely by clicking on **New Schedule**. The **Schedule Report** pop up shows us our options:

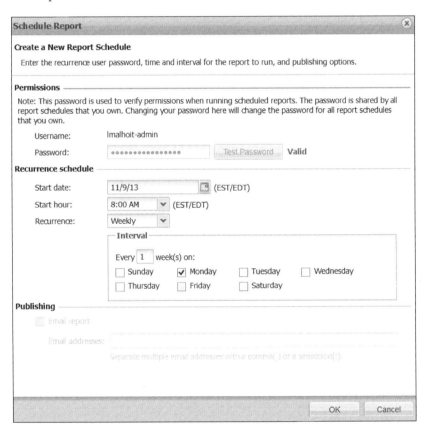

We only need to input our password, which we can test by pushing the **Test Password** button. We need proper admin permissions so the report will show us everything in our environment to which we have access. Then we can create the **Recurrence** schedule, which is pretty self-explanatory. Under the **Publishing** section, we see that everything is grayed out. We can enable e-mailing the report to people by configuring SMTP from the admin console. If we go to `https://<ip_address_of_ vC Ops>/admin` and click on the **SMTP/SNMP** tab, we can enter the information for our mail server, and the **Publishing** section will no longer be grayed out. Then we only need to click on **OK**, and the report will be e-mailed to the people we specify. To make it even easier, we can create distribution lists that can be altered outside of vC Ops, which will make it easier to manage. We don't have to e-mail the report. The report will be saved and listed with the date next to it, so we can always log in to the vC Ops UI to find it and then manually download the `.pdf` or `.csv` file.

# Understanding built-in reports

I've named built-in reports in the first section, but I think it's important to go through how to read the reports and use them to help us understand our environment. We'll go to the regular vC Ops UI under the **Reports** tab to get to these reports again. The first report we'll go through is the Virtual Machine Capacity Overview Report. Click on **Run Now** to get the report.

 If the report seems to be taking a while to generate, it's possible that it's actually done. If we click on the refresh icon, it will show the finished report with the PDF/CSV links on which to click.

# Virtual Machine Capacity Overview Report

The first page of every report is the title page that will look similar to this:

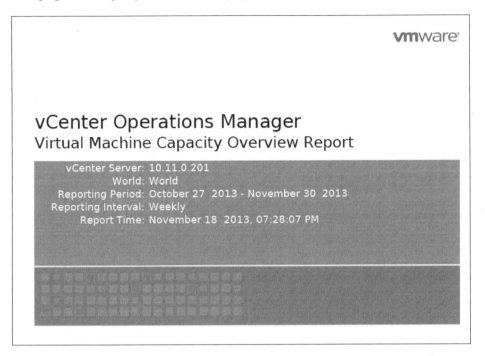

As we can see, it's branded with the VMware logo, and this can't be changed like the enterprise reports. It also tells us the name of the report we've run, which in this case is **Virtual Machine Capacity Overview Report**. It informs which vCenter Server this report correlates to. I've run this report with my **World** resource selected. We can also see **Reporting Period** and **Reporting Interval**, which can be changed in the **Configuration** area of vC Ops. Finally, we see **Report Time**, the time during which the report was run.

The next page on all of the reports is a table of contents as shown in the following screenshot. The table of contents will vary depending on the report we selected:

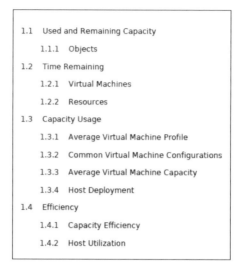

The next pages are a summary of what the report contains as well as a reminder of which policy is applied. If we're using the default policy (which we discussed in *Chapter 2, Installing vCenter Operations Manager*), or any policy for that matter, it will reflect the policy settings shown in **Configuration** as follows:

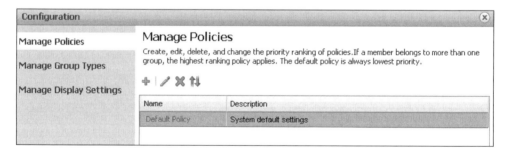

After that, we finally get to the meat of the report. As noted in our table of contents, the first part is **Trend and Forecast** for the **World** object:

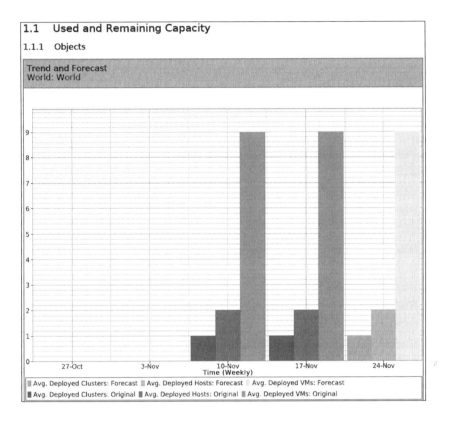

This graph shows us the previous weeks' trends as well as what the next week will look like if I continue with these trends. The graph shows I have one cluster that is being monitored with two hosts and nine VMs. If I continue this way, next week it is likely to look the same. If I start deploying more VMs, then the graph would adjust accordingly.

The next page is a similar looking graph done by objects, so I won't show it here. After that, we see the **Time Remaining** page that tells us how much time we have left for the VM capacity, given the current trends. In my example, it shows I have over a year left. On the next page, though, it breaks it down in a slightly better way for us. This should all look somewhat familiar as we can also see these results in some of the other tabs of vC Ops.

### 1.2.2   Resources

**World: World**

| | Time Remaining | Last 2 Weeks | Last Week | Current Week | Next Week | Next Month | Next Quarter | Next Half Year |
|---|---|---|---|---|---|---|---|---|
| Avg. Host CPU Effective Demand | > 1 year | - | 1,611 MHz | 1,005 MHz | 398 MHz | 0 MHz | 0 MHz | 0 MHz |
| Avg. Host CPU Reserved Capacity | > 1 year | - | 0 MHz | 0 MHz | 0 MHz | 0 MHz | 0 MHz | 0 MHz |
| Avg. Host CPU Allocation | > 1 year | - | 13 vCPU | 12 vCPU | 10 vCPU | 7.9 vCPU | 0 vCPU | 0 vCPU |
| Avg. Host Memory Effective Demand | > 1 year | - | 15 GB | 12 GB | 9.3 GB | 0.74 GB | 0 GB | 0 GB |
| Avg. Host Memory Reserved Capacity | > 1 year | - | 539 MB | 520 MB | 500 MB | 443 MB | 291 MB | 62 MB |
| Avg. Host Memory Allocation | > 1 year | - | 49 GB | 47 GB | 44 GB | 38 GB | 21 GB | 0 GB |
| Avg. Datastore Disk Space Total Used | > 1 year | - | 316 GB | 332 GB | 348 GB | 396 GB | 526 GB | 719 GB |
| Avg. Datastore Disk Space Allocation | > 1 year | 0.99 TB | 0.99 TB | 0.99 TB | 0.99 TB | 0.99 TB | 0.99 TB | 0.99 TB |
| Avg. Host Disk I/O Read | > 1 year | - | 127 KBps | 69 KBps | 11 KBps | 0 KBps | 0 KBps | 0 KBps |
| Avg. Host Disk I/O Write | > 1 year | - | 260 KBps | 140 KBps | 19 KBps | 0 KBps | 0 KBps | 0 KBps |
| Avg. Host Disk I/O Reads per Second | > 1 year | - | 3.3 Tps | 2.4 Tps | 1.4 Tps | 0 Tps | 0 Tps | 0 Tps |
| Avg. Host Disk I/O Writes per Second | > 1 year | - | 14 Tps | 10 Tps | 6.9 Tps | 0 Tps | 0 Tps | 0 Tps |

The first column shows us which resource it's referring to followed by **Time Remaining** for that resource. So, according to the trends, we currently have over a year left for all of our resources. Then again, we see **Last 2 Weeks**, **Last Week**, **Current Week**, and so on. Two weeks ago, I was not seeing many numbers in the column as this is a newer installation of vC Ops. The rest of the numbers show the actual utilization or resources in the past and the forecasted usage of resources in the future. This is not a highly utilized cluster yet. If I keep adding VMs, these numbers will change with time. As we scroll down to the next page, we see the **Average Virtual Machine Profile** screen:

## 1.3.1 Average Virtual Machine Profile

### World: World

| | Average | Standard Deviation |
|---|---|---|
| VM CPU Allocated | 1.5 vCPU | 0.035 vCPU |
| VM CPU Effective Demand | 121 MHz | 26 MHz |
| VM CPU Limited Demand | 50 MHz | 13 MHz |
| VM CPU Reservation Used | 0 MHz | 0 MHz |
| VM Memory Consumed | 3 GB | 279 MB |
| VM Memory Allocated | 5.4 GB | 27 MB |
| VM Memory Effective Demand | 983 MB | 147 MB |
| VM Memory Limited Demand | 551 MB | 47 MB |
| VM Memory Reservation Used | 55 MB | 0.6 MB |
| VM Configured Disk Size | 95 GB | 0 MB |
| VM Disk Space Usage | 41 GB | 739 MB |
| VM Disk Space Provisioned | 93 GB | 4.1 MB |
| VM Disk I/O Usage | 27 KBps | 6.4 KBps |
| VM Disk I/O Read | 7.5 KBps | 1.4 KBps |
| VM Disk I/O Write | 19 KBps | 4.9 KBps |
| VM Disk I/O Reads per Second | 0.27 Tps | 0.0059 Tps |
| VM Disk I/O Writes per Second | 1.1 Tps | 0.16 Tps |
| VM Network I/O Usage | 3.5 KBps | 2.2 KBps |
| VM Network I/O Received Rate | 2.1 KBps | 1.2 KBps |
| VM Network I/O Transmitted Rate | 1.7 KBps | 1.2 KBps |

To the left, we're shown a list of virtual machine resources and metrics. The middle column shows us the average usage of each resource. We're then shown **Standard Deviation**. A lower **Standard Deviation** means the data points collected were all somewhat close together. In this case, the Average column is pretty much on the point. If the Standard Deviation is higher, this indicates the Average in the middle should be considered as a representation, rather than a totally accurate figure. The Standard Deviation could possibly change the longer we have vC Ops up and running because of how vC Ops learns the environment.

In the following pages, we see many of the same graphs we've seen in previous chapters, such as Common Virtual Machine Configuration, Average Virtual Machine Capacity (trends and forecasts), Host Deployment, and so on.

# Oversized Virtual Machines Report

We described oversized virtual machines in *Chapter 5, Capacity Planning with vCenter Operations Manager*. This is the same thing that is shown by the **Planning** tab and the **Views** subtab, except in report view. Remember that we can have these reports scheduled and e-mailed to whomever we wish. So let's take a quick look at this report. The first few pages are similar to the other report in that we get a title page, table of contents, and summaries. Then, we're given the report of oversized VMs shown as follows:

## 1.1 Oversized Virtual Machines

**World: World**

| Virtual Machine | Policy | vCenter Server | Configured vCPU | Recommended vCPU | CPU Demand of Recommended (%) | Configured Memory | Recommended Memory |
| --- | --- | --- | --- | --- | --- | --- | --- |
| Analytics VM | Default Policy | VC55 | 2 vCPUs | 1 vCPUs | 7.4% | 9 GB | 2.8 GB |
| collector | Default Policy | VC55 | 2 vCPUs | 1 vCPUs | 1.6% | 3 GB | 0.16 GB |
| DC1 | Default Policy | VC55 | 1 vCPUs | 1 vCPUs | 1.4% | 4 GB | 0.34 GB |
| NSI-DC-01 | Default Policy | VC55 | 1 vCPUs | 1 vCPUs | 1.3% | 4 GB | 0.28 GB |
| NSI-EXCH-01 | Default Policy | VC55 | 2 vCPUs | 1 vCPUs | 21% | 4 GB | 2.6 GB |
| SQL | Default Policy | VC55 | 1 vCPUs | 1 vCPUs | 1.8% | 4 GB | 2 GB |
| UI VM | Default Policy | VC55 | 2 vCPUs | 1 vCPUs | 27% | 7 GB | 2.5 GB |
| VC55 | Default Policy | VC55 | 1 vCPUs | 1 vCPUs | 26% | 4 GB | 1.3 GB |
| vCSA | Default Policy | VC55 | 2 vCPUs | 1 vCPUs | 4.5% | 8 GB | 1 GB |

In the first column, we see the virtual machine's name. We're then shown the policy that's applied to it as configured in the configuration as well as the vCenter Server we are connected to. The fourth column shows how many vCPUs it has followed by the recommended vCPU. The **CPU Demand of Recommended** column tells us how many of the recommended vCPUs we're actually using. Then, we see the **Configured Memory** and **Recommended Memory** columns we can get away with going down to without impacting the VM.

In the **Planning** tab and the **Views** subtab, we can see undersized VMs in the **Undersized Virtual Machines Report** as well.

# Capacity Inventory and Optimization Report

If we want to see oversized VMs, undersized VMs, as well as other inefficiencies in the environment all within one report, we can run the Capacity Inventory and Optimization Report. This report starts with listing **Capacity Optimization Candidates** that lists **Total Virtual Machines**, **Powered-Off Virtual Machines**, **Undersized Virtual Machines**, and **Idle Virtual Machines**.

### 1.1    Capacity Optimization Candidates

#### 1.1.1    Virtual Machine Optimization

**World: World**

|  | VMs |
|---|---|
| Total Virtual Machines | 9 |
| Powered-Off Virtual Machines | 0.0 |
| Undersized Virtual Machines | 0.0 |
| Oversized Virtual Machines | 9.0 |
| Idle Virtual Machines | 4.0 |

On the following pages, we see more detailed information about each of these categories, starting with Idle Virtual Machines. This table lists compute resources and disk space usage for each VM vC Ops considered to be idle. As we can see in the following screenshot, the idle times for **CPU**, **Disk**, and **Network** are all very close to 100 percent:

#### 1.1.2    Idle Virtual Machines

**World: World**

| Virtual Machine | Policy | vCenter Server | CPU Demand | CPU % Idle Time | Disk I/O Usage | Disk I/O % Idle Time | Network I/O Usage | Network I/O % Idle Time | Memory Consumed | Total Virtual Disk Space Configured | Provisioned Disk Space |
|---|---|---|---|---|---|---|---|---|---|---|---|
| collector | Default Policy | VC55 | 7.4 MHz | 100% | 0.38 KBps | 100% | 0.04 KBps | 100% | 0.51 GB | 16 GB | 19 GB |
| DC1 | Default Policy | VC55 | 13 MHz | 100% | 4 KBps | 98% | 0.038 KBps | 100% | 2 GB | 50 GB | 54 GB |
| SQL | Default Policy | VC55 | 2.7 MHz | 100% | 0 KBps | 100% | 0 KBps | 100% | 0.03 GB | 100 GB | 104 GB |
| UI VM | Default Policy | VC55 | 55 MHz | 99% | 19 KBps | 97% | 0.75 KBps | 93% | 4.5 GB | 132 GB | 139 GB |

The next page shows us **Oversized Virtual Machines** tables, which I won't show again, as it's the same table as the one shown earlier in the *Oversized Virtual Machines Report* section. We can also see the **Undersized Virtual Machines** table that shows the percentage of undersized CPUs as well as the percentage of undersized memory. The last table is **Powered-Off Virtual Machines**, which is a list of VMs that are powered off, the disk space they're using, and the percentage of time during which they've been powered off.

# Average/Peak Datastore Latency and Throughput Report

Let's take a look at the **Average/Peak Datastore Latency and Throughput** report:

## 1.1 Average/Peak Datastore Latency and Throughput

| World: World | | | | | | | | | | | | |
|---|---|---|---|---|---|---|---|---|---|---|---|---|
| Object | Policy | vCenter Server | Powered On VM Count | Write Latency( Average) | Write Latency( Peak) | Workloa d @ Max Write Latency | Read Latency( Average) | Read Latency( Peak) | Workloa d @ Max Read Latency | Through put(Aver age) | Through put(Peak ) | Capacity Risk @ Max Through put |
| VMDatas tore2 | Default Policy | VC55 | 1.4 | 0.26 ms | 0.55 ms | 5 | 0.89 ms | 3.7 ms | 7.2 | 77 KBps | 543 KBps | 92 |
| VMDatas tore1 | Default Policy | VC55 | 2.9 | 0.16 ms | 0.35 ms | 7 | 0.18 ms | 3.5 ms | 7 | 52 KBps | 624 KBps | 86 |
| VMDatas tore3 | Default Policy | VC55 | 5.3 | 0.03 ms | 0.25 ms | 5.1 | 0.52 ms | 5.1 ms | 5.1 | 117 KBps | 644 KBps | - |

In the first column, we see **Object**, in this case, the datastores. Again, we see **Policy** and **vCenter Server**. The fourth column shows us the **Powered On VM Count** which are the powered-on VMs on that datastore. We then see our **Write Latency (Average)** and **Write Latency (Peak)**. They look pretty good here as I don't have many VMs on datastores. However, if we're seeing averages of over 20 to 30 ms, we might want to check for other alerts in our dashboards. Even something over 5 ms might be worth checking out. This will be different in every environment and for different applications though. Just keep in mind, the higher the latency, the longer it will take for an I/O to complete the operation. Perhaps if we have other datastores with less latency, we may want to move VMs off the busy datastores to other datastores. If we don't have that option, we may want to consider purchasing more storage. This is pretty much the same for Read Latency as well. For both Read and Write Latencies, we can see the Workload score at peak times of latency. The last few columns refer to Throughput. Throughput is basically the data transfer speed or the rate at which data can be transferred from one device to another. The last column shows us our Capacity Risk score when the Throughput is at its peak.

# Health Score and Alert Trend Report

The Health Score and Alert Trend Report is a great report to receive on a scheduled basis, and we can receive it for different sites or the **World** object (or really any object at all). If we look at the graph shown in the following screenshot, we see what the health of the World object is:

We see the familiar vertical line dividing our past and present from the future, or rather **Current** from **Forecasted**. The first graphed element we see is **Badge | Health: Trend**, or if we want to refer to it in a normal way, it's basically the trend of the Health Badge Score. On 27 October, it was around 85 or so, and as of 17 November, it rose to around 94. If it stays with this trend, it will keep rising as shown in the **Forecasted** section. This is good news because as we recall, we want the Health Score to be as close to 100 as possible.

The rest of the graphed elements are pretty similar. They're all pretty close to zero, which is also good news, because if we look through what they are, they're all different types of alerts such as **Critical, Immediate, Warning,** and so on. The less alerts we have, the better our environment is.

Also, the Health Score and Alert Trend Report will give us the hard numbers as shown in the following screenshot:

### 1.1  Health Score and Alert Trend

**Alert count**
World: World

| Time | Badge \| Health | Trend | Badge \| Alert Count Critical | Trend | Badge \| Alert Count Immediate | Trend | Badge \| Alert Count Warning | Trend | Badge \| Alert Count Info | Trend |
|------|------|------|------|------|------|------|------|------|------|------|
| Week Starting 27 Oct, 2013 | - | 84 | - | 3 | - | 0 | - | 2 | - | 0 |
| Week Starting 3 Nov, 2013 | - | 87 | - | 2 | - | 0 | - | 1 | - | 0 |
| Week Starting 10 Nov, 2013 | 90 | 90 | 2 | 2 | 0 | 0 | 1 | 1 | 0 | 0 |
| Week Starting 17 Nov, 2013 (This Week) | 92 | 92 | 1 | 1 | 0 | 0 | 0 | 0 | 0 | 0 |
| Week Starting 24 Nov, 2013 | - | 95 | - | 0 | - | 0 | - | 0 | - | 0 |

The first column tells us the time period with the first row being a few weeks back and the last row being the next week after the current (future). We can see what our Health Badge scores were each week. We then see the **Trend** column that shows us the same numbers as the graph on the previous page did. It goes on to show us how many different alerts there are and what the trend is for those as well.

# VM Average and Peak Storage Access Latency Report

The VM Average and Peak Storage Access Latency Report is similar to the Average/Peak Datastore Latency and Throughput Report, but it's broken down by VMs.

## 1.1   VM Average and Peak storage access latency

**World: World**

| Object | Policy | vCenter Server | Avg. Write Latency(ms) | Peak Write Latency(ms) | Workload @ Max Write Latency | Avg. Read Latency(ms) | Peak Read Latency(ms) | Workload @ Max Read Latency |
|--------|--------|----------------|------------------------|------------------------|------------------------------|-----------------------|-----------------------|-----------------------------|
| NSI-DC-01 | Default Policy | VC55 | 0.87 ms | 1.6 ms | 10 | 0.64 ms | 3.3 ms | 12 |
| vCSA | Default Policy | VC55 | 0.22 ms | 0.43 ms | 8.4 | 0.5 ms | 2.5 ms | 7.3 |
| DC1 | Default Policy | VC55 | 0.18 ms | 1.7 ms | 5.6 | 0.26 ms | 1.3 ms | 12 |
| UI VM | Default Policy | VC55 | 0.13 ms | 0.46 ms | 26 | 0.41 ms | 0.93 ms | 22 |
| collector | Default Policy | VC55 | 0.1 ms | 1.1 ms | 7.7 | 0.27 ms | 0.73 ms | 10 |
| NSI-EXCH-01 | Default Policy | VC55 | 0.079 ms | 0.19 ms | 40 | 2.4 ms | 4 ms | 46 |
| VC55 | Default Policy | VC55 | 0.041 ms | 0.25 ms | 20 | 0.43 ms | 5.1 ms | 20 |
| Analytics VM | Default Policy | VC55 | 0.033 ms | 0.32 ms | 16 | 0.55 ms | 1.2 ms | 32 |
| SQL | Default Policy | VC55 | - | - | - | - | - | - |

This is an interesting table because it shows not only the Read and Write Latency but also what each VM has for a Workload score during peak times. Keep in mind these Workload scores are not necessarily an average but is an interesting piece of information. If we see some of them getting up closer to 100, we might want to take a look at the resources assigned to them and whether the latency is affecting the application enough that users are complaining.

# Custom Reports

Now we have custom reports only offered in the Enterprise version. To get to these reports, we go to `https://<ip_address_of_vC Ops>/vC Ops-custom`. There is a **REPORTS** tab, as shown in the following screenshot, that gives us the option to create pretty specific reports from all the metrics vC Ops collects:

Here we see **CORRELATION** and **ADVANCED**. There are three kinds of correlation reports: performance, behavior, and anomaly. The advanced reporting contains the option to upload a default report. Uploading a default report gives us the option to upload a `.jpg` file that would most probably be a logo of our company. Using this allows us to put our own brand on the custom reports before printing them out or e-mailing them.

Follow the given steps to upload an image:

1. Open the custom dashboard by going to `https://<ip_address_of_vC Ops>/vC Ops-custom`.

2. Log in as an admin or some other user we've set up as an administrator.

3. Navigate to **REPORTS | ADVANCED** and select **Upload Default Report Image**.

4. Select the header image by clicking on **Browse** and then selecting the `.png`, `.gif`, `.jpeg`, or `.jpg` file of our company.

5. Click on **Upload**.

6. Once we click on **Upload**, the **Current Header Image** will change to the image we've selected and the image will appear on our reports:

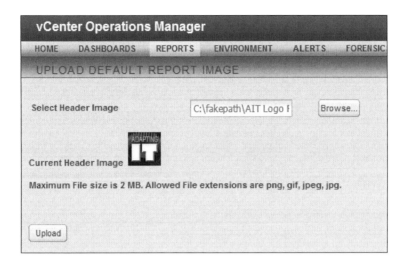

The Performance Correlation report, as shown in the following screenshot, lets us see how the performance of one metric correlates with another:

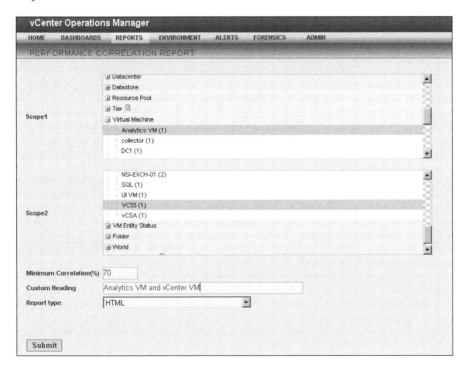

In this report, we choose a resource from **Scope1** and **Scope2** along with a **Minimum Correlation** percentage. We can choose multiple resources from each scope. If we choose multiple resources, it will match up everything. In other words, it's an AND rather than an OR. The default **Minimum Correlation** is **70%**, but we can choose anything from 50 percent, if we are okay with a lower correlation, to 100 percent for the highest correlation. We can then give the report a heading and choose whether we'd like it to be **HTML**, **PDF**, or **CSV**. For these reports, remember to turn off our pop-up blocker if we chose **HTML** as it will pop up as another web page.

The **BEHAVIOR CORRELATION REPORT** is similar in that we pick two resources, but we can only compare two at a time. We can see whether the two resources are having similar symptoms or behaviors:

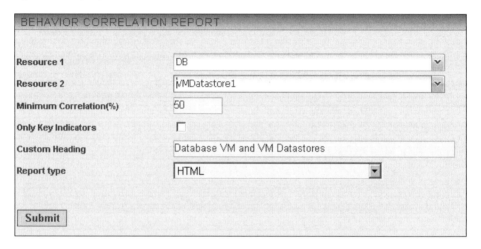

Finally, we have the Anomaly Correlation Report that looks almost exactly like the Behavior Correlation Report but tells us which anomalies two resources have in common. If we've configured **Key Performance Indicators (KPIs)**, we can put a check in the box to make sure we're only looking at the resources and metrics we've selected as KPIs. We can again give them both custom headings and select a report type.

To really use these reports, let's think about a situation where we have a proprietary application that we run in our environment. This application VM has a database backend, as so many do, on a different VM. If we choose **Resource1** to be one of the application VMs and **Resource2** to be our database VM, we can see whether there have been any similar symptoms or anomalies between the two. We can also do this with the Performance report, but we can even specify all of our application VMs in Scope1. If we don't see any problems there, we would want to run the reports with one of the datastores or hosts perhaps to see whether there are any correlations there. It's not that we couldn't find this information within the dashboards in the custom or regular UI, but it's not spelled out for us within the same spreadsheet. By using the correlation reporting, we can get these answers quickly and perhaps see things that we wouldn't have seen by looking for them manually.

# Summary

In this chapter, we went over the difference between custom (only available to enterprise users) and built-in reports. These reports can be scheduled to run routinely or run quickly to see the state of our environment at any point in time. Many of the metrics shown in the reports are available in other tabs of the vC Ops UI, but the reports give us a nice deliverable to print or e-mail.

In the next chapter, we'll start discussing how vCenter Operations Manager can be used and integrated with other products such as vCenter Configuration Manager. This chapter will go over a basic installation of the vCenter Configuration Manager as well as how to hook it in to vC Ops.

# 7
# vCenter Configuration Manager

In this chapter we'll learn the following topics:

- Basic vCenter Configuration Manager installation
- How to connect vCenter Configuration Manager and vC Ops
- How to use vCenter Configuration Manager with vC Ops

**vCenter Configuration Manager** (**VCM**) is a solution that allows companies to automate and keep track of configuration compliance and change management. It will keep the data of changes made within the environment as well as alert admins of machines that fall outside defined compliance rules. It can even revert configuration changes made from within VCM automatically so that machines become compliant again. VCM will also work with vC Ops, so we can tell in detail what kinds of changes have caused problems within our environment.

# Basic vCenter Configuration Manager installation

VCM is a very complicated solution, and any advanced installation configurations are outside the scope of this book. We will go through a basic installation in this chapter so as to get started with using VCM with vC Ops.

Please see the vCenter Configuration Manager installation guide for more information on installation found here: `http://www.vmware.com/pdf/vcenter-configuration-manager-57-installation-guide.pdf`.

In order to install VCM, we will need a Windows 2008r2 VM and at least two domain accounts (one interactive account and one service account), which will both need to be local admins on the VCM VM. Once we have these requirements in order, we'll get started with the *Typical* (also called *Single Tier* or *Basic*) install.

A typical installation can be done by using the following steps:

1.  Login as the administrator account we plan on using for the VCM.

2.  Download the ISO file from `vmware.com`, and attach it to the Windows 2008r2 VM we've created for VCM.

3.  Click on the Typical Install option.

4.  We'll see a **EULA** which we'll need to accept before moving on.

5.  Run the pre-requisite check. If we want to see the full results of the check, we need to put a checkmark next to **View Full Results**. This will appear as a pop up in another browser page as shown in the following screenshot.

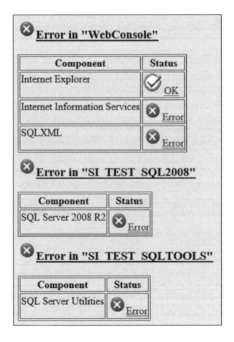

6. We don't necessarily need to view the full results though, because the next screen in the wizard also tells us what pre-requisites aren't yet met and allows us to install them.

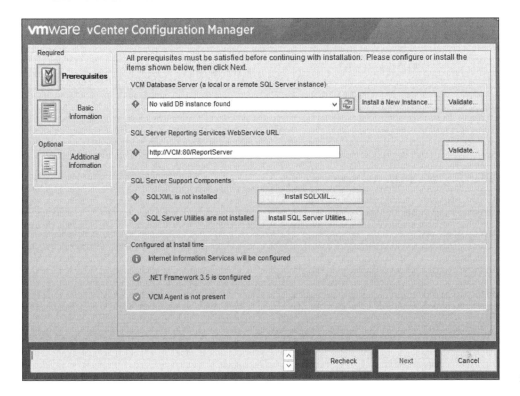

7. As shown in the previous screenshot, we're missing several pre-requisites starting with a SQL server instance. In newer versions, we can actually install SQL right from this wizard, provided we have SQL server installation files.

8. To install SQL, click on the **Install a New Instance** button, and then browse to the SQL installation directory. This installation can take quite a few minutes.

9. When we install SQL, it will take care of the **VCM Database Server, SQL Server Reporting Services WebService URL**, and **SQL Server Support Components**. We can install SQLXML by clicking on **Install SQLXML** and then clicking on **Download** and finally **Install**.

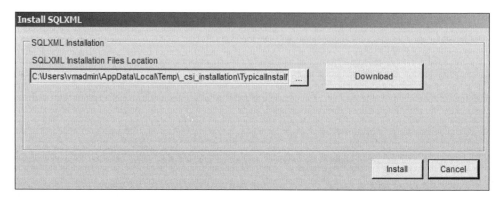

10. Click on **Next** after all the pre-requisites have been installed.

11. On the next screen, we'll type in our license keys and click on **Add** to validate them. Notice that in the bottom left of the wizard there is a running list of tasks that have been completed. We can refer to this list to make sure everything has been completed successfully.

12. We'll also enter our VCM service user created earlier here and click on **Validate** to make sure it works. Make sure this is a different account than the account we're logged in with.

13. We'll leave the install path as the default in this example. We'll also leave the **HTTPS** option checked to maintain a secure connection. For this example, I'll leave it as a self-signed certificate, but it's encouraged to use a certificate from a certificate authority to maintain integrity.

14. Once we've completed that screen, we'll click on **Install**. At this point, **IIS (Internet Information Services)** will be automatically configured.

15. When the installation is complete, we'll put a checkmark next to **Launch VCM Web Console on Exit** and click on **Exit**.

# VCM basic configuration

VCM is a really complex product that's capable of doing many things. So we will be sticking to the basic configuration to show how it can be useful with vC Ops here as well. Once we login to VCM by browsing to `https://<IP_of_VCM>/vcm`, we see the following **Console**. It shows us a brief description of each tab available to us through the UI.

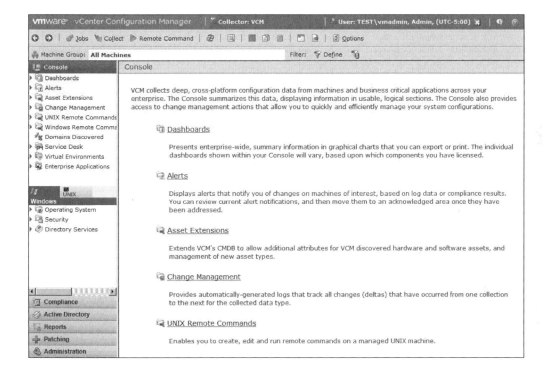

Here is a flowchart of our next steps:

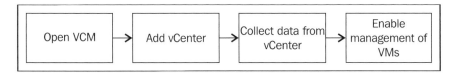

The first thing we need to do, since our typical installation has taken care of much of the component configuration, is to add our vCenter server to VCM. To add our vCenter server to VCM use the following steps:

1.  Click on the **Administration** slider on the left.

2.  Click on the **Available Machines** tab under **Administration**.

3.  Click on the **Add Machines** link.

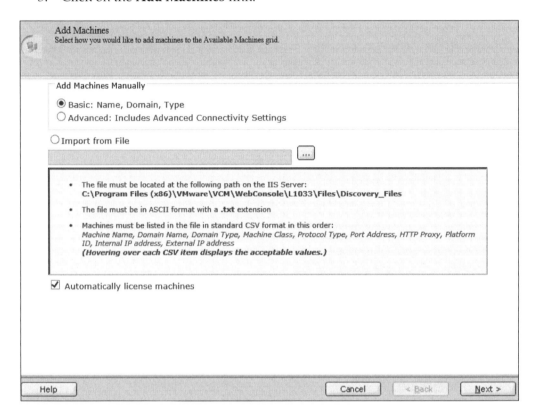

4.  Select **Basic** to add the machines manually, and click on **Next**.

5. On the next screen, you'll add our vCenter server by entering its host name next to **Machine, Domain, Type**, and **Machine Type** and then clicking on **Add**. Make sure you select **vCenter (Windows)** as **Machine Type**.

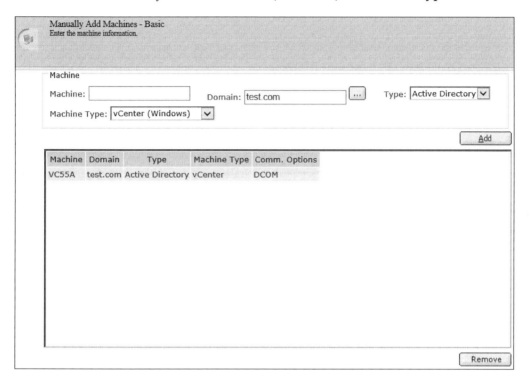

6. Click on **Next** and then on **Finish** to complete the task.

7. Now expand **Licensed Machines**, and click on **Licensed Virtual Environments**.

8. Highlight our vCenter VM, and click on the **Configure Settings** button at the top.

9. Click on **Next** on the **Virtual Environment** screen.

10. On the **Managing Agent and Communication Settings** screen, we need to specify **Managing Agent**, which will just be our VCM server in this case. We can create other agents depending on the size of our environment. Then we'll need to add a username and password to connect to vCenter.

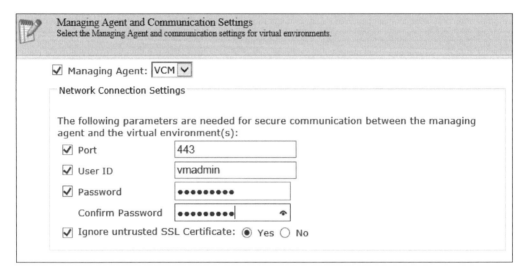

11. Click on **Next** and then on **Finish**.

12. Back on the main VCM screen, we'll click on the **Collect** button on the global toolbar at the top to collect data from our vCenter server.

13. As the **Collection Type**, just select **Machine Data**, and then click on **OK**.

14. Make sure the vCenter server is in the **Selected** category on the **Machines** screen, and then click on **Next**. We'll leave the rest of the options as default.

15. On the next page, expand **Virtualization** and select the options that align with our virtual infrastructure. We can select all of them, but if we don't use vShield or vCloud Director for instance, there's no sense in trying to collect that data.

The collection can also be configured as a scheduled task and probably should be used to keep information up to date. For more information on this, please see the vCenter Configuration Manager administration guide:

`http://www.vmware.com/pdf/vcenter-configuration-manager-55-administration-guide.pdf`

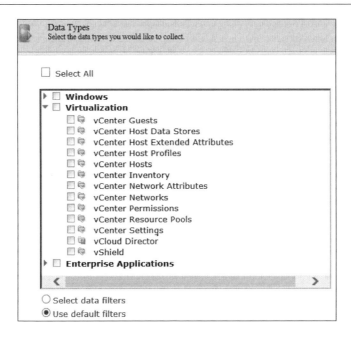

16. Click on **Next** to check if there are any **Conflicts**. If not, click on **Finish**.

17. If we click on the **Jobs** button up in the global toolbar, we can see if the job has been finished and if all the tasks were completed successfully.

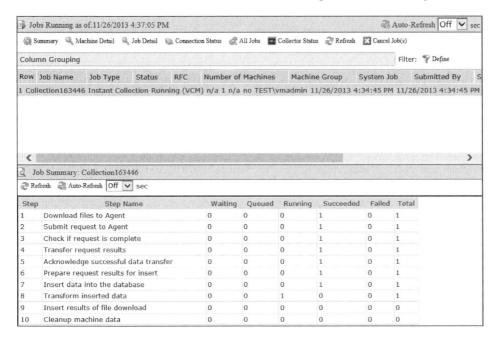

18. When the job is finished, we can go to the console slider on the left-hand side and expand **Virtual Environments**. If we click through the various sub tabs of **Virtual Environments** we can see that information has been collected.

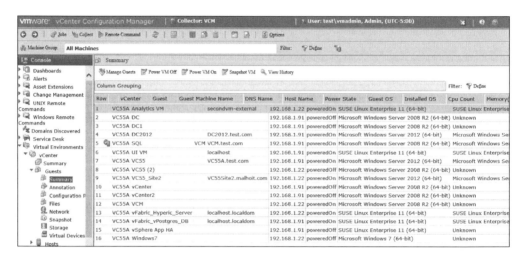

Now that we have our Virtual Environment set up within VCM, we need to be able to manage the VMs. This will give us the ability to do things such as power on or power off VMs, take snapshots, and so on. Use the following steps to manage VMs:

1. While we're still in the **Console** slider, we'll expand the **Guests** sub tab and click on **Summary** as shown in the previous screenshot.

2. Select the VMs we'd like to have managed by clicking on them. We can use *CTRL* or *Shift* to select more than one VM at the same time.

3. Click on the **Manage Guests** button at the top to bring up the wizard.

4. Put in **Domain**, select the **Domain Type**, and then click on **Next**.

5. If we need to edit any of the VM information, we can do so on the next screen.

6. On the **License VM Guests** screen, put a check next to **License the Selected Machines** and **Install VCM Agents for the selected Windows machines**. We also need to make sure that we're very careful about this. If we select the wrong machines, we may accidentally apply the incorrect configuration options.

7. Click on **Next** and **Finish**.

# Connecting VCM and vC Ops

vC Ops is able to use adapters to connect to other VMware and third-party solutions to collect more metrics and relationships. Some adapters, such as vCenter Server and vCenter Configuration Manager, are built into the vApp. However, if we're using the standalone installation of VCM, we will need to download and install it.

Adapters talk to the *Collector* , which is built into the Analytics VM of the vApp. Since the vCenter Configuration Manager is built-in, it's fairly simple to connect to vC Ops.

Use the following steps to connect VCM to vC Ops:

1.  Open a browser and connect to the admin UI at `https://<vC Ops_IP_Address>/admin`.

2.  Scroll to the bottom of the **Registration** tab, and click on the **New Registration** button.

3.  Fill out the fields in the **vCenter Configuration Manager Registration** screen according to the information for our VCM server. The user account that we use here cannot be an interactive account. Use a service account dedicated to VCM, such as the service account created at the beginning of the chapter.

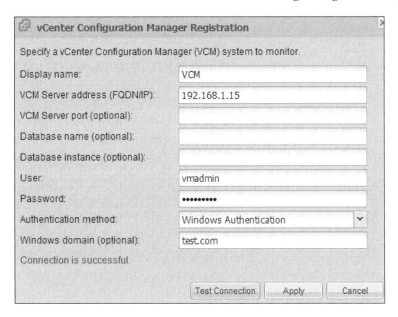

4.  We can then test the connection by clicking on the **Test Connection** button. If we've entered the information properly, we will see **Connection is successful** in green at the bottom under **Windows domain**.

5. Click on **Apply** to finish.

6. If that's successful, we will now have a VCM instance within our vC Ops environment as shown in the following screenshot:

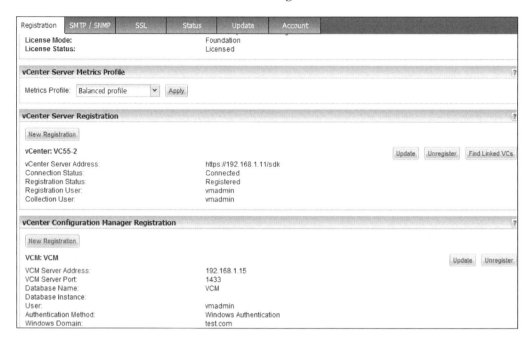

We will now need to configure VCM to report to vC Ops. There are two settings that we can collect from VCM, which are **Change Events** and **Standards Compliance**. Change Events records when something is changed and by whom if the change was made from VCM, while Standards Compliance reports back to vC Ops about the servers and devices that are not within our compliance rules. Use the following steps to configure VCM to report to vC Ops:

1. Open a browser, and go to our VCM portal.

2. Click on the **Administration** slider, and navigate to **Settings**.

3. Click on **Integrated Products**.

4. Click on **VMware**.

5. Select **vCenter Operations Manager**.

6. Click on **Change Events**.

Here we see many metrics we can report back to vC Ops, such as **Unix Patch Assessments** and **Windows Software Inventory**.

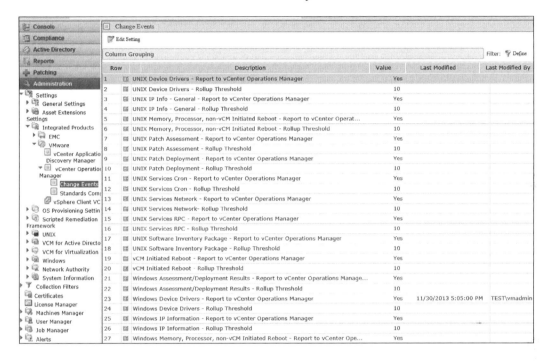

By highlighting one of the rows, we can edit it by clicking on **Edit Setting**. We can then change the setting to communicate with vCenter Operations Manager. It will also tell us when this was **Last Modified** and who modified it.

Now we can click on **Standards Compliance** on the left-hand side. We see a similar screen. We see many of the descriptions include the words **Badge Risk**. Values here can be pulled into vC Ops and used to calculate a more accurate risk score as long as VCM and vC Ops are collecting from the same vCenter servers. Since guest agents may have been installed as well, vC Ops will gather metrics on the guest operating systems as well.

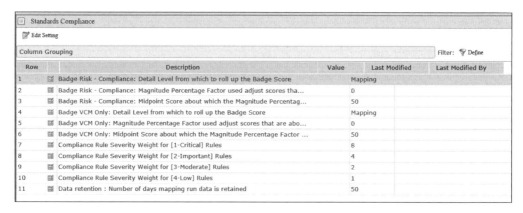

In order to really use VCM, we will need to configure compliance rules; otherwise how would we know we're not within compliance? So our next step will be to create rules and templates, which we'll go through briefly here.

First we'll create a rule using the following steps:

1. Click on the **Compliance** slider.

2. Expand **Virtual Environment Compliance**.

3. Expand **Rule Groups**.

4. Click on **Rules**.

5. Click on the **Add** button at the top to create a new rule.

6. Give the rule a name and description. For this example, I'm going to create a rule to ensure that *VMware Tools* are running. So I'll call it *VMware Tools Rule*.

7. On the **Data Type** screen, expand **Virtualization**, and put a check next to **vCenter – Guests – Summary**.

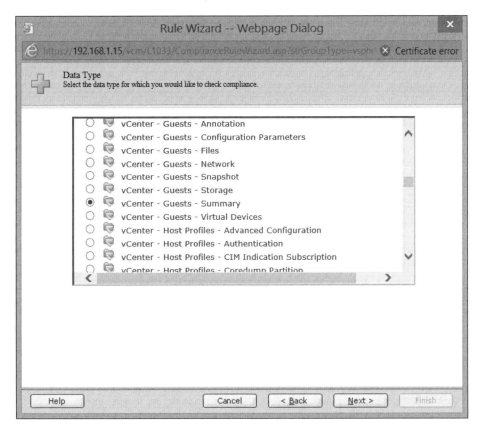

8. On the **Rule Type** screen, we'll select the **Basic** type.

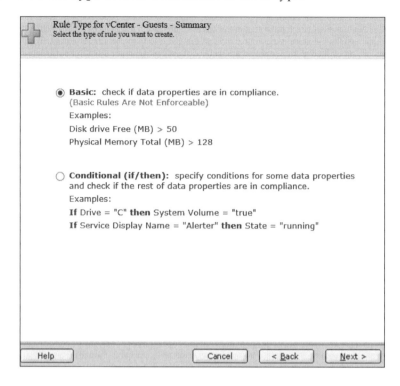

9. On the **Basic Properties** screen, click on the **Add** button.

10. Select the **Tools Running Status** from the drop-down menu.

11. Make sure the **=** sign is also selected.

12. Click on the ellipsis to select the **guestToolsRunning** property.

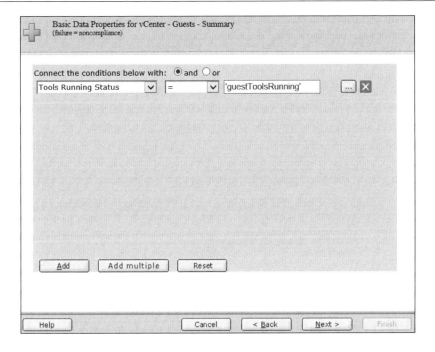

13. On the **Options** screen, click on the severity you'd like to choose: **Critical**, **Important**, **Moderate**, or **Low**.

14. Click on **Finish** on the following screen to add the rule.

The rule will now appear under **Compliance Rules**. As shown, we can **Preview**, **Edit**, **Clone**, **Move**, **Copy**, **Delete**, and **Set the Order** of, the rules in this list.

We'll now create a template that we can apply to our environment using the following steps:

1. While still under the **Compliance** slider and **Virtual Environment Compliance**, highlight **Templates**.

2. Click on the **Add** button to create a template.

3. Give the template a name and description. In this example, we'll call it *Compliance Rule Template*.

4. On the next screen highlight compliance rule, and press the right arrow to move it to the right column.

5. On the **Template Options Screen**, select **Return both compliant and non-compliant**.

6. On the last screen, click on **Finish** to create the template.

Now that we have rules and templates configured, we can create **Compliance Badge Mappings**. This will allow us to apply templates and configure how the score is calculated. We can also use the Content Wizard tool to download other compliance templates created by VMware.

>  The Content Wizard tool can be found by going to the Start menu on the VCM server and navigating to VCM Tools. We can download various templates, such as up-to-date vSphere Hardening Guides, PCI templates, and Sarbanes-Oxley Templates, from the Internet. We simply select the templates we want, and click on Install. It will take several minutes, but after they're installed, they will appear in the mappings like any other template.

To create a mapping, use the following steps:

1. While still under the Compliance slider, click on **vCenter Operations Manager Badge Mapping**.

2. Click on **Mappings**.

3. Click on **Add**.

4. Give the mapping a name and description, and select **Virtual Object Group Compliance**, which is where we'll find the template we've created. If you'll notice, next to **Badge** it says **Risk – Compliance**, which is what we want.

5. On the **Machine Groups** screen, we'll select **vCenter Guest Machines**.

6. On the select **Compliance Template(s)** screen, we'll double click on the templates we want to include within this mapping.

7.  Then we'll click on **Finish**, and the mapping will be added to the list.

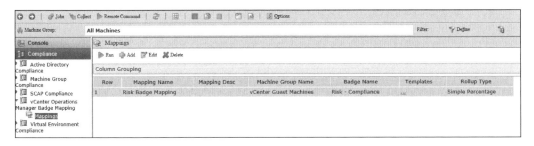

When we've created the mappings we need, also schedule this to run routinely. We can again do this under the **Administration** slider using **Job Manager**.

# Using VCM metrics within vC Ops

At this point, we've spent a lot of time in VCM, and most likely we'll be spending even more time tweaking it so that it does everything we need it to do within our environments. Now we can jump back into our vC Ops dashboard to see some of the VCM metrics and how they affect our badges.

# Compliance

As I mentioned previously, the Risk badge will be the most affected by VCM when it comes to compliance. In fact, we have a new minor badge called **Compliance** under the **Risk** badge as we can see in the **Dashboard** tab.

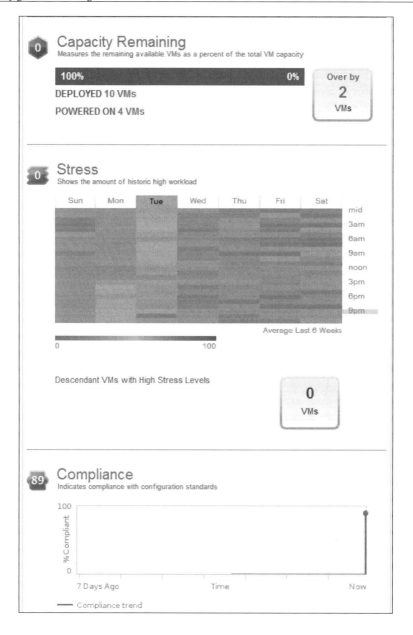

**Compliance** will be a score between 0 and 100, with 100 meaning that our object(s) are completely compliant when compared to the templates we've chosen. When we click on the Compliance score, we're taken to the **Planning** tab under the **Views** sub tab. As shown in the following screenshot, there is a new view called **Compliance Breakdown**.

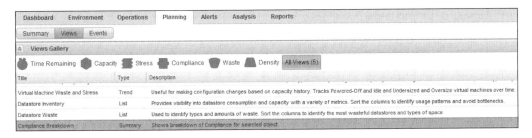

We can pick any object on the left-hand side from our tree, and we can see how it compares with our different templates. In the following example, we're looking at how a VM compares with the multiple compliance templates that have been mapped from VCM.

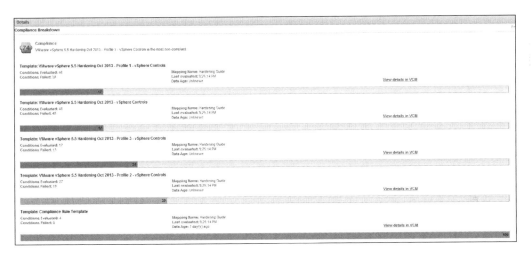

We can see which template it's being compared with. We see the **Compliance** score for this VM is **74** in total. Below that, we see each template and a breakdown of how compliant the VM is with each template. Red means we're not very compliant; yellow is a warning; and green means we're very compliant. Though we don't get a description of how this is calculated within vC Ops, we can click on the link that says **View details in VCM** to get this information. In this example all the templates are calculated the same way; however, within VCM, we can give different weights to different mappings if some of the templates are more important than the others. Our rules can also affect the score if we assign one rule as Critical and another as Moderate.

# Change events

If we click on the **Events** sub tab under the **Planning** tab, we can see that the **Compliance** minor badge is here too. If we highlight an object on the left-hand side and click on the **Compliance** minor badge, we see a graph with change events and other compliance issues.

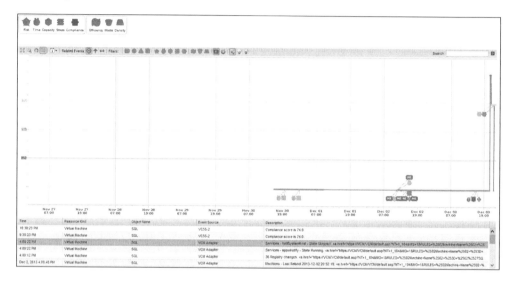

We can click on the events in the graph, and they will appear highlighted in the list below. Right now, we see the change event highlighted where a service was stopped. Notice that the **VCM Adapter** is listed as the **Event Source**. Others could show if the VMware Guest Tools are running or if the VM was powered on. We can also see the Compliance score and when or if that changed. We can then go into VCM to get more detailed information such as who made the change and we can even roll it back if we'd like to from the VCM console.

# Summary

We've been over a typical vCenter Configuration Manager setup and also how to connect vC Ops to VCM. Once it was all connected, we saw how VCM inserts a Compliance badge into our vC Ops UI. We can see change events and compliance rules for any object within our virtual environment as long as we have proper rules, templates, and mappings. Some of the templates can be downloaded from VMware and third-party sources, while others can be created by the administrator.

The Compliance score ultimately affects the Risk major badge, but keep in mind that a lot of this is user defined. So, be careful while mapping templates if they're not applicable or perhaps should be weighted less than other templates. VCM is a pretty complicated solution in that there is just so much to it. It would be highly recommended to research VCM thoroughly before applying any changes to our production environment.

Even more value is offered by the integration and use of vC Ops with VCM. Take the example of seeing a VM in vC Ops with a low Health score. When we drill into that VM within vC Ops, we might see that the CPU is running really high. Then from the Events tab, we find something like an antivirus software installation. We can go directly into VCM and see when it happened and who did it. We can also revert the changes automatically if VCM initiated the change. This provides a very efficient way of correcting issues within our environment.

In the next chapter, we'll be going over how VMware Log Insight can integrate with vC Ops. Log Insight is a tool used to aggregate server logs as well as analyze and monitor servers within our environment. We'll go over how to install and connect it to vC Ops and then find out how it can be used within vC Ops to obtain even more metrics.

# 8
# Log Insight

Log Insight is a **Security Information and Event Management (SIEM)** solution offered by VMware that was released in 2013. It will parse and aggregate Windows and Linux logs from your VMware guests as well as objects such as ESXi hosts, datastores, and third-party solutions with proper configuration. Instead of realizing that a problem exists in your environment and going through each log on each server individually, we will be able to navigate to one spot and intelligently search for errors. Log Insight can also notify us when problems arise. With proper logs at our finger tips, we should be able to identify and solve issues quickly and efficiently.

Log Insight is not part of the vCenter Operations Suite currently. It is licensed by all operating systems, meaning we pay by each device from which it collects the logs. For instance, if we wanted to collect logs from eight VMs and two hosts, we would need to pay for 10 devices.

You'll learn about the following topics in this chapter:

- Installing and configuring VMware Log Insight
- Connecting Log Insight to vCenter Operations Manager
- Using Log Insight with vCenter Operations Manager

## Installing and configuring Log Insight

Log Insight comes as a virtual appliance or an `.ova` file. A virtual appliance is downloaded from VMware, or sometimes through a third-party vendor, and deployed directly from vCenter. It's generally a locked-down operating system with preinstalled software. All we need to do is provide details such as networking information. If you'd like to download and try it before you buy, there is an evaluation version available.

If you'd like to learn more about Log Insight or get an evaluation, you can go to `http://www.vmware.com/products/vcenter-log-insight/`.

The following steps will help you install Log Insight:

1. Download the Log Insight `.ova` file from VMware.

2. In the vCenter web client, click on **Hosts and Clusters**.

3. Right-click on the top level of the **Hosts and Clusters** screen and click on **Deploy OVF Template**.

4. Click on **Local File**, and then browse to the Log Insight virtual appliance that was just downloaded, and click on **Open**.

5. Click on **Next** on the **Review Details** screen.

6. Accept the EULA and click on **Next**.

7. Enter a name and choose a location where we'd like the appliance to be located:

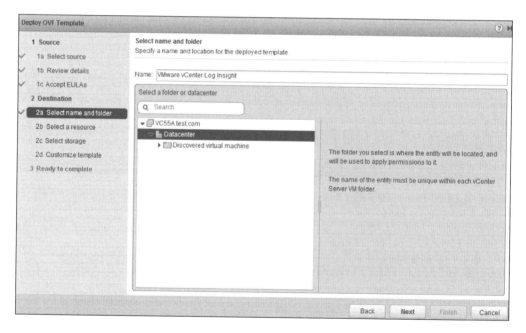

8. Select a resource on the next screen, which will generally be a cluster, host, or a resource pool.

9. Select whether we would like to deploy it as thin or thick provisioned. Thin provisioning will allow us to over-allocate our datastore if we don't plan on using all of the storage. Thick provisioning will take up all the space allocated to the virtual appliance immediately. Usually, in production environments, we choose thick provisioning so it doesn't start chewing up our entire datastore without us realizing it.

10. Choose a datastore on this screen as well and click on **Next**.

11. Enter the network information, including Default Gateway, DNS server, and the IP address for Log Insight.

12. Specify a hostname and click on **Finish**. Then, power on the appliance.

When the appliance is powered on, we see a screen that will look similar to the following screenshot:

```
VMware vCenter Log Insight 1.0.4 Build 1169900


Visit VMware vCenter Log Insight:
http://192.168.1.16/




To access the console, use CTRL+ALT+F1.
    - If using a Windows keyboard, press WindowsKey+Alt+F1
      or press Ctrl+Alt+Space, then release the spacebar while
      holding down Ctrl+Alt, and then press F1.
    - If using a Mac keyboard, press Fn+Ctrl+Alt+F1.
    - If the above key combinations do not work, check your keyboard mapping.

To switch back to this screen, use CTRL+ALT+F2.
    - Use the above key combinations but replace F1 with F2.
```

From this screen, we see that to manage Log Insight, we need to open a browser and go to `http://<Log_Insight_IP_Address>`. We can also go to the console by pressing *Ctrl + Alt + F1*. We may need to use the key combinations described in the screenshot to make it work. To continue with the setup, we'll browse to the Log Insight IP address.

The following steps will help you proceed with the initial configuration:

1. Open the browser and go to `http://<Log_Insight_IP_Address>`.

2. Upon our first visit, we see a welcome screen, and we need to click on the **Next** button to begin.

3. On the next screen, we need to enter an e-mail address and password for our admin credentials as shown in the following screenshot:

4. On the next screen, enter a license key and click on **Set Key**.

5. On the **General Configuration** screen, enter an e-mail address where we want to receive notifications.

6. We need to configure time information on the next screen. Check the times to make sure they're correct. We can either sync them with an NTP server or an ESXi host. Then, enter the NTP Servers information and click on **Test**:

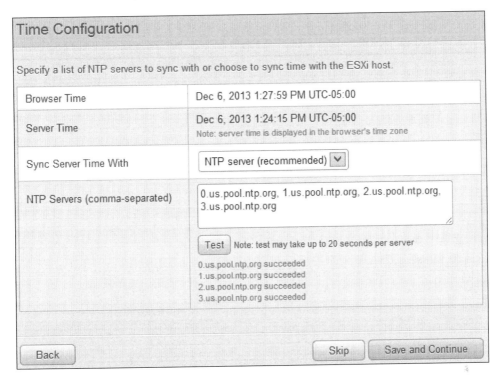

## Time Configuration

Specify a list of NTP servers to sync with or choose to sync time with the ESXi host.

| Browser Time | Dec 6, 2013 1:27:59 PM UTC-05:00 |
|---|---|
| Server Time | Dec 6, 2013 1:24:15 PM UTC-05:00<br>Note: server time is displayed in the browser's time zone |
| Sync Server Time With | NTP server (recommended) ▼ |
| NTP Servers (comma-separated) | 0.us.pool.ntp.org, 1.us.pool.ntp.org, 2.us.pool.ntp.org, 3.us.pool.ntp.org |

Test  Note: test may take up to 20 seconds per server

0.us.pool.ntp.org succeeded
1.us.pool.ntp.org succeeded
2.us.pool.ntp.org succeeded
3.us.pool.ntp.org succeeded

Back                                    Skip     Save and Continue

7. On the **SMTP Configuration** page, enter the IP address or FQDN of our SMTP server so we can receive e-mails from Log Insight. We can also enter an e-mail address to test whether it will work.

8. The next part is important: VMware Integration Configuration. On this screen, we need to put a checkmark under **Enabled** for **vCenter Server**, enter the hostname for our vCenter server along with credentials, and click on **Test**. Make sure the test is successful. By enabling vCenter integration, we'll get tasks and events from vCenter logged within Log Insight in real time:

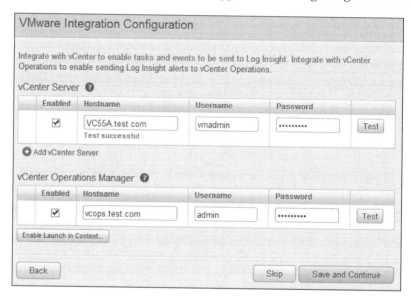

9. While still on the preceding screen, put a checkmark under **Enabled** for **vCenter Operations Manager**. Enter the hostname and credentials for vC Ops and again click on **Test**. If the test is successful, click on the **Enable Launch in Context** button. This will enable our usage of Log Insight within vC Ops.

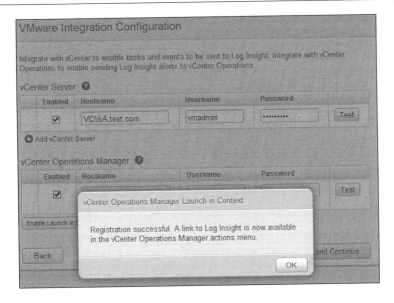

10. The next screen allows us to enable archiving. Put a checkmark next to **Enable Data Archiving** if we would like to save older logs to a different location via NFS:

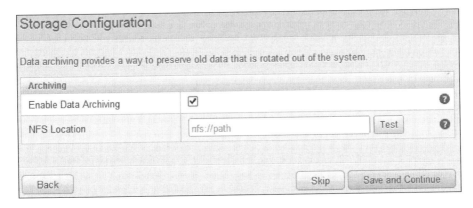

11. On the **Restart Required** screen, click on **Restart**. This will restart the Log Insight service, not the entire virtual appliance.

So now we see a screen similar to the one that follows. It's fairly empty because we haven't configured anything to report to it yet. This will be the next step in our configuration.

To start collecting event logs and data, follow the given steps:

1. Log in to the console by using root as the user and leave the password blank.

2. When it asks for the old password, leave that blank as well.

3. Create a new password that has an uppercase letter, lowercase letter, number, special symbol, and is of at least eight characters. After we've configured a new password, we can use Putty or another SSH client to log in to the machine. SSH is disabled until a new password is created though.

4. Enter the following command to collect host events and be sure to change the credentials to what we've set up within our environment. The username and password referenced in the following example is for our vCenter server:

```
Configure-esxi --username admin --password p@ssw0rd --server
<vcenter IP address> --target udp://localhost:514
```

Log Insight has a built-in syslog server, which is what we're specifying with the `--target` switch in the previous command. It listens over TCP/UDP 514 as well as TCP 1514 for SSL connections.

5. We see the following information for each host within the environment:

```
Configuring hosts connected to vc55a.test.com to send logs to udp://localhost:51
4

NOTE: configure-esxi will work methodically but not quickly. Large inventories
or slow network connections will further slow down execution. Please be patient.

Attempting to connect to vCenter Server vc55a.test.com

Host: 192.168.1.91, VMware ESXi 5.5.0, 1331820
Old Syslog.global.logHost: "192.168.1.24"
New Syslog.global.logHost: "192.168.1.24,udp://localhost:514"
Changes successful.

Host: 192.168.1.22, VMware ESXi 5.5.0, 1331820
Old Syslog.global.logHost: ""
New Syslog.global.logHost: "udp://localhost:514"
Changes successful.
```

At the time of writing this, Log Insight Version 1.04 is the latest GA release. The public beta for 1.5 is currently available though, and it makes adding ESXi servers a little easier because we can add them from the GUI. See the following screenshot for advanced ESXi configuration options from the GUI:

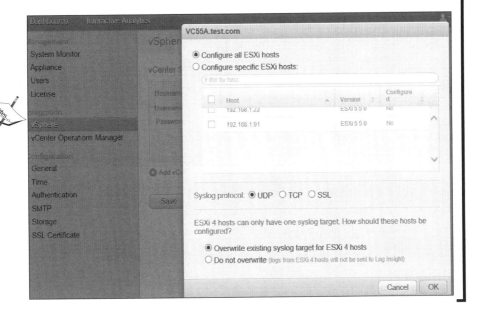

6.  That's all we need to get going. Log Insight uses what VMware calls content packs to create rules and policies that go into collecting and analyzing certain event data. It comes with a built-in vSphere content pack. We can create our own content pack or download it from the VMware Marketplace. Current content packs include Cisco UCS, EMC VNX, NetApp, VMware Horizon View, Puppet Enterprise, and so on.

If for some reason we get locked out of Log Insight during the setup or we can't remember the password, there is a way to reset the password from the console. Most of the workings of this method are taken from *VMware vCenter Log Insight Installation and Administration Guide*.

Open the vSphere client and log in to the Log Insight console using root. Enter the following command to get the salt for the admin password:

```
./psql -d logdb -U liuser -p 12543 -c "select * from li_
user where name ='admin';"
```

We then need to hash the salt to get the password:

```
PASS='echo -n "SALTFROMABOVE" | sha256sum | cut -d " " -f
1'
```

 Now we need to make it so that logging into Log Insight via the GUI will prompt us for a new password:

```
./psql - d logdb -U liuser -p 12543 -c "update li_user
set password='$PASS' where name='admin';"
```

In the guide, it does say that we will be prompted for the `liuser` password. However, the guide doesn't seem to tell us what the `liuser` password is. Through trial and error, I've found that if you use liuser as the password as well this will work, at least in the current 1.04 Version.

Once we run the command successfully, we can then log back into Log Insight, and it will take us through the configuration wizard again where we can change the password. There is also a script you can download from this link: `http://loginsight.vmware.com/a/dtd/Reset-admin-password-command-line-script/13833-24427`

# Using Log Insight with vC Ops

In Log Insight, we automatically receive logs; however, just because we've connected it to vC Ops doesn't mean it is sending alerts over there automatically. We can do it with any alert that comes up in Log Insight. Let's look at a security use case for this. Log Insight can detect if someone tries to log in to an ESXi host with the wrong username and password. Let's go through setting it up to see it in vC Ops as well.

First we'll click on the **Interactive Analytics** button to see the following screen:

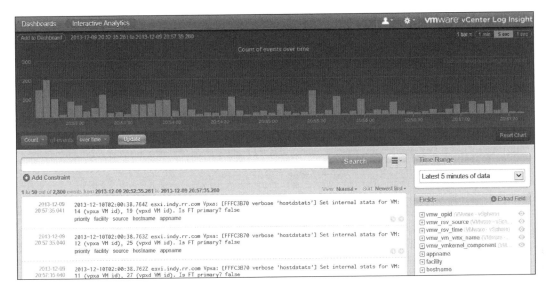

The top of the screen shows us a graph with all of the logged data we've collected. We also have a **Search** field that allows us to search for events based on keywords. To the right, we can change **Time Range** to whatever period we want. Under the **Fields** table, we can expand each **Extract Field** to see the metrics that pertain to it. For instance, if we expand **hostname**, we can see the metrics broken up by each host within our environment as shown in the following screenshot:

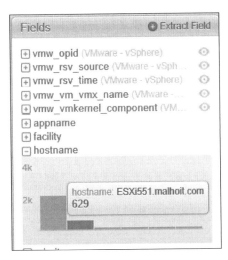

Now that we've gone through the initial tour, let's jump into our scenario. If we click on the button right next to the **Search** field, we see the option to manage alerts and we can click on it. Then, we'll click on **ESX/ESXi: Unsuccessful Authentication** shown as follows:

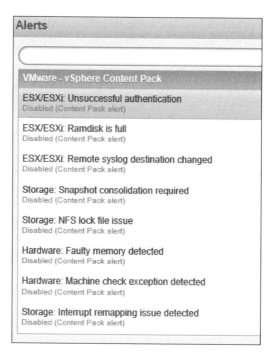

This brings us to the **Add Alert** screen where we can put in a name, notes, and enable the ability to send the alert to vC Ops. We can also enable sending an e-mail when an alert is triggered here.

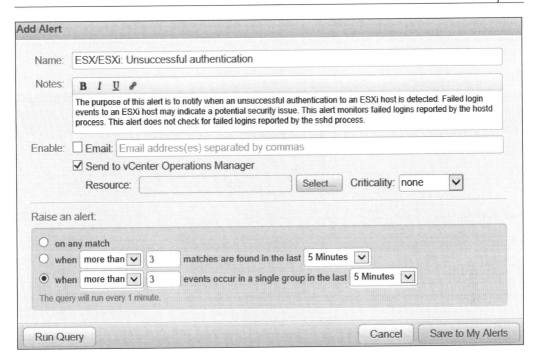

We need to put a check next to **Send to vCenter Operations Manager** to have the alert sent. Next we'll select the resource we'll assign it to and then assign the **Criticality** level. In this case, I'm going to assign an ESXi server, because that's what someone is trying to log in to, as the resource and assign it the Criticality level of critical. We then want it to raise an alert when this happens more than three times within five minutes. These options can all be changed as well. Then we'll click on the **Save to My Alerts** button to enable this alert.

Now we can find the alerts in a couple of ways. If we go back to **Manage Alerts**, we can click on the **Run Query** button that will bring up the alerts that match this information. We can also just type in `password for user` in our **Search** field to find the information:

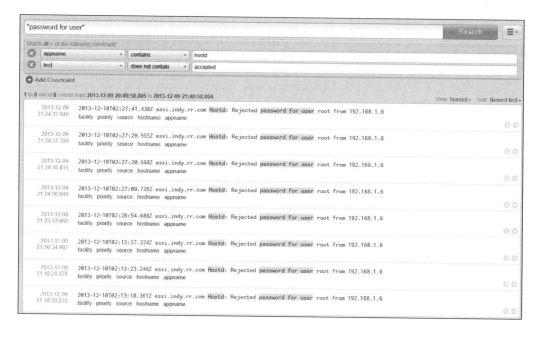

We can now open our vC Ops UI to find this alert. In the tree to the left, we'll click on the host that someone's been trying to log in to. Then we'll click on the **Operations** tab and select the **Events** subtab. The **Health badge** should be selected by default; if not, we can go ahead and select it. We now have a new icon, an orange circle with a yellow triangle on it; we can choose to turn on notification alerts as shown in the following screenshot:

If we turn it on by clicking on the icon, we'll see the notification events as shown in the following screenshot:

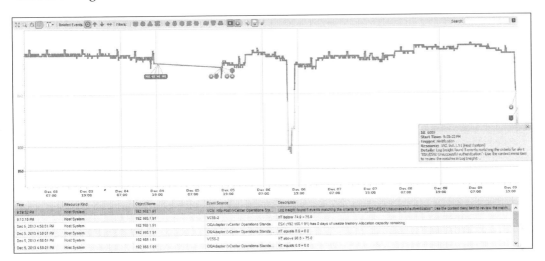

If we click on one of the notification events on the graph, the following message will appear:

**Details: Log Insight found 5 events matching the criteria for alert "ESX/ESXi: Unsuccessful authentication": Use the context menu item to review the matches in Log Insight.**

We can then click on the **Actions** button at the top of the screen and select **Search for logs in vCenter Log Insight**. This is where the **Enable Launch in Context** button comes in which we configured during the installation. With this enabled, we can search for events directly in Log Insight from the vC Ops UI. It will bring up the Log Insight UI with the appropriate search:

Let's take a look at another example. Perhaps we've been seeing slower performance for VMs on a certain datastore. We suspect there's some latency on one of the datastores, so we set up an alert in Log Insight to be warned when the logs reflect this latency. This time let's type in `latency` in the **Search** field under **Interactive Analytics**. We'll assign it a name such as `Storage Latency` and tell it to send an alert to vCenter Operations Manager as we did before.

This time we'll go into our vC Ops custom UI to see what gets reported. First, we'll click on the **Alerts** tab and then highlight the offending datastore.

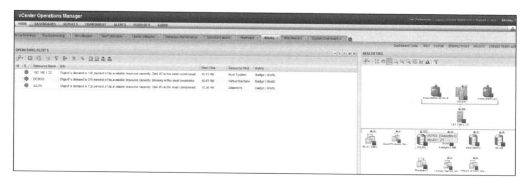

Then we can click on the show alerts icon represented by a red triangle with an exclamation point in it. The following screenshot gives us a list of alerts for that particular object, in this case a datastore:

| Criti... | Type | Sub... | Start Time | Resource Name | Metric | Alert Info |
|---|---|---|---|---|---|---|
| ⚠ | Ⓒ | Ⓐ | 11:05 PM | iSCSI1 | | Log Insight found 10 ... |
| ⚠ | Ⓒ | Ⓐ | 11:00 PM | iSCSI1 | | Log Insight found 10 ... |
| ⚠ | Ⓒ | Ⓐ | 10:55 PM | iSCSI1 | | Log Insight found 10 ... |
| ⚠ | ■ | ▲ | 10:53 PM | iSCSI1 | Badge \| Anomaly | High number of metric... |
| ⚠ | Ⓒ | Ⓐ | 10:53 PM | iSCSI1 | Badge \| Anomaly | HT above 77.0 > 75.0 |
| ⚠ | Ⓒ | Ⓐ | 10:48 PM | iSCSI1 | Badge \| Health | HT below 12.0 < 25.0 |
| ⚠ | ■ | ✿ | 10:38 PM | iSCSI1 | Badge \| Workload (%) | Object's demand is 1... |
| ⚠ | Ⓒ | Ⓐ | 10:38 PM | iSCSI1 | Badge \| Workload (%) | HT above 138.0 > 95.0 |
| ⚠ | ★ | ⌚ | 12/2/13 11:4... | iSCSI1 | Badge \| Time Remaini... | DATA STORE (iSCSI1... |
| ⚠ | ★ | ● | 12/2/13 11:4... | iSCSI1 | Badge \| Capacity Rem... | DATA STORE (iSCSI1... |
| ⚠ | Ⓒ | Ⓐ | 12/2/13 11:4... | iSCSI1 | Badge \| Risk | HT equals 100.0 = 100.0 |
| ⚠ | Ⓒ | Ⓐ | 12/2/13 11:4... | iSCSI1 | Badge \| Capacity Rem... | HT equals 0.0 = 0.0 |
| ⚠ | Ⓒ | Ⓐ | 12/2/13 11:4... | iSCSI1 | Badge \| Time Remaini... | HT equals 0.0 = 0.0 |

We'll then double-click on one of the alerts that says **Log Insight within the Alert Info**:

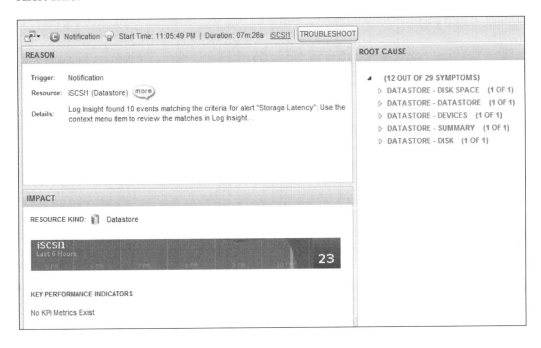

Again, in the **REASON** section next to details, we see that Log Insight found these events. We can also click on the icon at the left uppermost part of the screen and click on **View notification in vCenter Log Insight**. This will again allow us to Launch in Context and pull up the search from within the Log Insight UI:

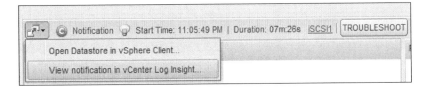

# Summary

In this chapter, we learned how to install VMware vCenter Log Insight, which is a downloadable virtual appliance from VMware. It collects logs and provides a place to analyze them in real time with abilities to search and categorize. Log Insight uses content packs to collect certain kinds of data from various operating systems including servers, storage arrays, network switches, and so on. The vSphere content pack is built-in and available immediately. Other content packs can be downloaded from the VMware Marketplace.

Log Insight can also be integrated with vCenter Operations Manager during the initial setup or after it has already been configured. We can add alerts that will be triggered when particular logs are parsed, and these alerts can either be e-mailed to administrators or they can be sent over to vC Ops. If we look in vC Ops, we can see these notification alerts both in the regular and custom UI. This also works the other way around. If we see alerts in vC Ops, we can click on them to launch them in the Log Insight UI using the Launch in Context technology.

In the next chapter, we'll go over using vC Ops with VMware Horizon View. vC Ops, before the Horizon View plugin, has typically been ignorant of the VDI environment. Now that we have a view adapter, we can actually find metrics not only for VMs but the actual pools and other resources particular to the Horizon View.

# 9
# VMware Horizon View Integration with vCenter Operations Manager

VMware Horizon View, heretofore referred to as View, is a **virtual desktop infrastructure (VDI)** solution that's part of Horizon Suite. View allows administrators to centrally manage end user devices as well as ensure security and data loss protection. View can automatically provide pools of desktops to end users on physical devices, such as desktops, laptops, and tablets. It will work via a client installed on the end user device as well as via a web browser. Monitoring View with vC OPS can only be done with the Enterprise version of vC OPS as it uses the custom UI.

The topics that you'll learn in this chapter are:

- High-level installation overview
- Connecting Horizon View with vC OPS
- Exploring View dashboards
- Practical uses

# High-level installation overview

View can be a very complex solution to install correctly. There are multiple components to consider, and it requires a lot of design work before we actually get to the installation. Design and installation of the entire View product is outside of the scope of this book. However, we will go through some of the components needed, and what they do, so that we can understand what we need to monitor and troubleshoot within vC OPS.

The components are as follows:

- **View standard server**: This is sometimes referred to as a connection server sometimes. This provides the management GUI, or View Manager, for things such as pool creation as well as acting as a broker to create VMs via vCenter and serve out desktops to end users. We, as administrators, will spend most of our time here. It can be installed on a Windows server.

- **View security server**: This server generally sits in a DMZ and allows users that are outside the network to connect into the network securely. It's really the same download from VMware as the Connection Server, but while installing it, we choose **View Security Server** instead as shown in the following screenshot:

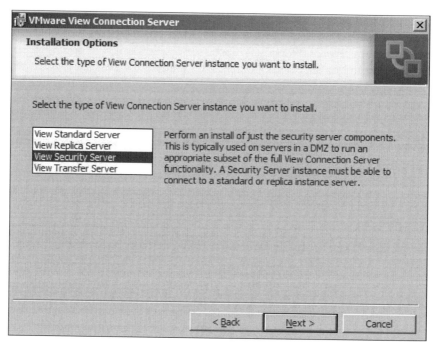

- **Replica server**: This is optional, but in most cases, we will need redundancy and load distribution among connection servers. This will quickly install a new connection server and import data from the current environment. This could also possibly be used for upgrading the underlying operating system with minimal or no downtime to the View environment.

- **Transfer server**: This is also an optional server. It will only be used in cases where we have local mode desktops (desktops available offline). This server is essentially a holding place for local mode desktops.

These four components will allow us to get started with Horizon View. In the examples provided in this chapter, we'll be assuming that there is one security server and one connection server. Though in most configurations we'll have at least two of each depending on the number of desktops. Again, having at least two of each server provides us with redundancy and load-balancing capabilities. Within the management of View, we have various components that make up the VDI infrastructure explained as follows:

- **Desktops**: These are virtual machines with desktop operating systems. These will be pushed out to the end users.

- **Pools**: These are groupings of virtual desktops with the same operating systems, appliances, and updates/patches. We can have multiple pools within the environment.

- **Persistent disks**: There are a couple of ways to deploy desktops. We can make them non-persistent, so every time a user logs off, the information is flushed, and we get a brand new desktop. We can also have persistent desktops. Persistent disks within the virtual desktops will retain data and generally be dedicated to a specific user. Persistent disks are where the retained data is stored on each desktop.

- **ThinApps**: These allow us to create virtualized applications and actually stream them into desktops if we choose to. This makes it easier to deploy and maintain applications from a central location.

- **Event database**: View comes with an option to configure an Event database that will store historical errors within the View environment. This needs to be configured separately and is not necessary for View to work. However, it is wise to configure it in the case that we're using the vC OPS adapter for View to get more information in vC OPS.

In the following screenshot, we can see the **VMware Horizon View Administrator** portal where we can manage our servers as well as the pools, desktops, and so on.

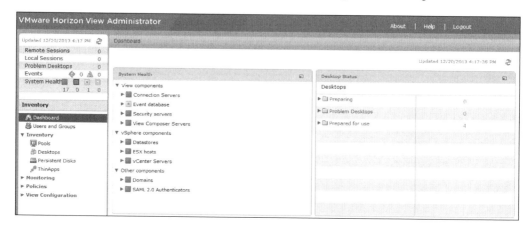

Although we have some monitoring capabilities from within the View Administrator UI, it's not extensive. Mostly it tells us about errors on the desktops. We cannot see any performance metrics here. We can look in vCenter for performance metrics, but unless we have View on its own hardware cluster, it might be time consuming to get this information. Even if we have it on its own hardware cluster, as is usually recommended, finding metrics such as what's provided via vC OPS would be difficult.

# Configuring the Event database

The Event database is optional but useful for vC OPS, so we'll go through the installation process here:

1. Create a database on our preferred database server. Make sure we know the login information. We'll want to use SQL authentication.

2. Log in to the View Admin UI by opening a browser and going to `https://<view_IP>/admin`.

3. Expand **View Configuration** under the **Inventory** section.

4. Click on **Event Configuration**.

5. Click on the **Edit...** button.

6. The **Edit Event Database** window pops up.

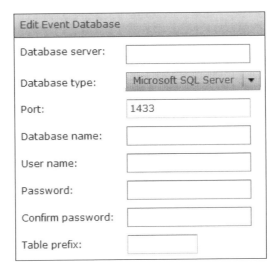

7. Fill out the information to reflect our environment.

8. Click on **OK**. The UI will let us know if the Event database is configured successfully. The Event database can tell us things such as if desktops are failing to provision or if there is an authentication issue.

If we're using SQL as the database, make sure it is set to connect via port 1433 and that the TCP/IP ports are both active and enabled. For more information and troubleshooting, see *VMware View KB 1029537* at `http://kb.vmware.com/selfservice/microsites/search.do?language=en_US&cmd=displayKC&externalId=1029537`.

# Connecting Horizon View with vC OPS

The vC OPS for View option has three main components: the adapter, the broker agent, and the desktop agents. In View 5.2 and above, the View agents includes the vC OPS desktop agent. The adapter is part of vC OPS or a vC OPS collector, and the broker agent allows the desktop agents and the collector to communicate. We'll be using View 5.2 for this configuration. With earlier versions the installation becomes a little more involved.

The steps to install vC OPS for View are as follows:

1.  Download the VMware vC OPS for Horizon View Adapter from VMware.

2.  Log in to the vC OPS admin portal at `https://<vC OPS_ip_address>/admin`.

3.  Click on the **Update** tab, and browse for the adapter's `.pak` file we just downloaded.

4.  Click on **Update**.

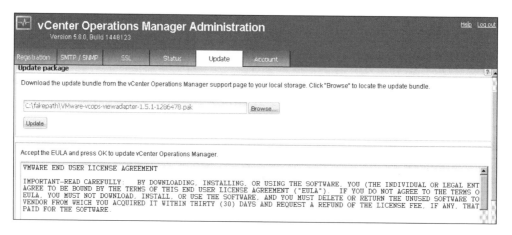

5.  Accept the EULA to continue, and then click on **OK**.

6.  After a few minutes, we'll see that the update has completed successfully. There's no need to log out and log in again for this update.

7.  If we then log in to the custom UI by browsing to `https://<vC OPS_IP_address>/vC OPS-custom` and hover over the **Admin** tab, we can select **Support**. Then click on the **Info** tab, and we can see that our View adapter is listed as V4V. V4V stands for vC Ops for View.

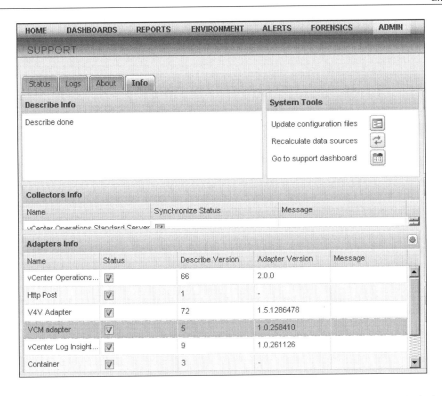

8. While still in the custom UI, hover over the **Environment** tab, and click on **Configuration** and then on **Adapter Instances**.

9. We need to add a new adapter instance for the View adapter by clicking on the add adapter instance icon.

10. First we select which collector we'll be using. If we don't have any additional collectors, we'll just see vCenter Operations Standard Server.

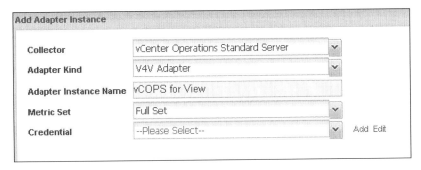

11. Select **V4V Adapter** in the **Adapter Kind** drop-down field.

12. Give it a name under **Adapter Instance Name**.

13. Either choose **Full Set** or **Reduced Set** for the **Metric Set** field. Full set will report on all of the metrics available.

14. We'll need to add **Credential**, so we'll click on the **Add Edit** link.

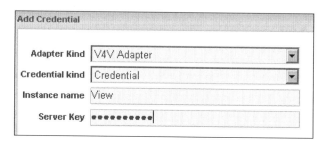

15. The **Adapter Kind** field will again be **V4V Adapter**.

16. Choose **Credential** for the **Credential kind** field.

17. Specify **Instance name**.

18. Specify **Server Key**, which will later be used to pair the broker agent with the adapter, and then click on **OK**.

19. Click on **Test** present on the **Add an Adapter Instance** screen to confirm success, and then click on **OK**.

We'll now need to download the VMware vC OPS for Horizon View's broker agent on View Standard Server. If we have multiple servers, we'll need to install it on all of them. Once the agent is downloaded on View Standard Server, we can start the installer by following the given steps:

1. Run the install, click on **Next** through the wizard, and then click on **Install**.

2. Leave **Launch the vCenter Operations Manager for Horizon View Configuration Utility** checked.

3. Click on **Finish**, and then we see the **Configuration Utility** window pop up.

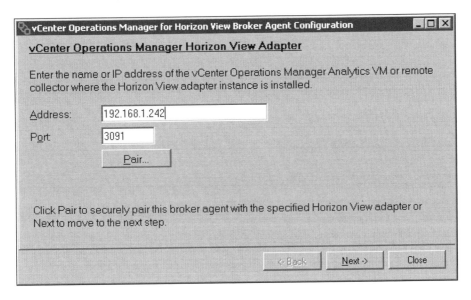

4. Enter the IP address of the Analytics VM.

5. The port is prepopulated with 3091.

6. Click on **Pair**.

7. Enter the server key we specified when we created the adapter instance, and click on **OK**.

8. A window will pop up, telling us if the pairing was successful. Click on **Close**.

9. Click on **Next**.

10. If we have an older version, we can import data on the next screen. If not, leave it blank, and click on **Next**.

11. On the next screen, we'll put in the credentials for the Event database we configured earlier. We'll again get a pop up that tells us it was successful.

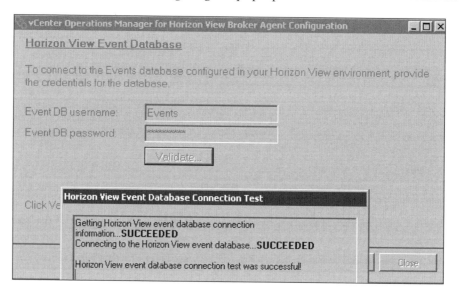

12. Click on **Next** to configure the pools we want to monitor.

13. We can optionally put in the name of our pools on this screen. We get the name from the View Admin UI.

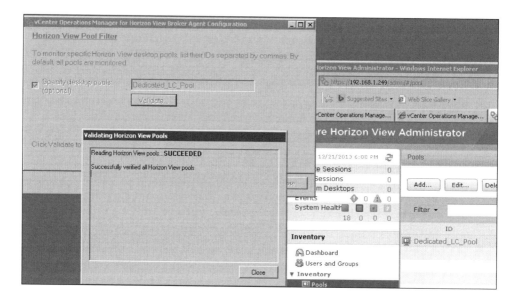

14. Click on **Next**, and then click on **Finish** to complete the Configuration utility.

15. We're then shown the Broker Agent Settings where we can change everything we just configured as well as things like the logging level.

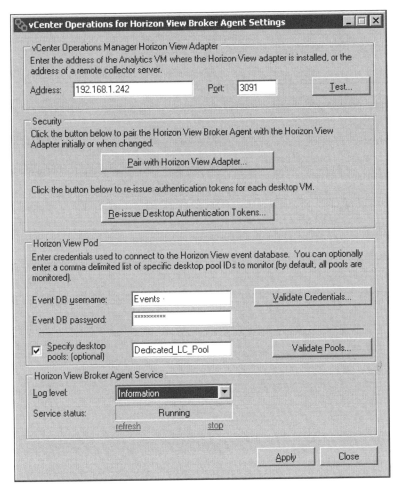

16. Click on **Apply** if we make any changes; otherwise, click on **Close**.

That's the entire install for View 5.2 and above. We can now log in to the vC OPS custom UI to see our View dashboards.

# Using vC OPS for View

There are seven dashboards that come with vC OPS for View. The first one that we see is **View Main**.

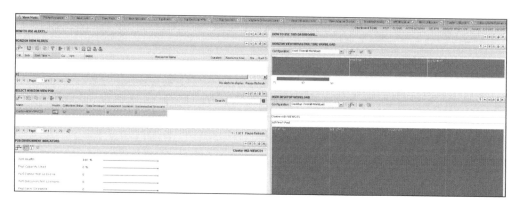

In the top left of the screen, we see the active alerts within the View environment. Below that, we see health and connection status sorted by pod. **Pod** is the term used by VMware to refer to sets of connection servers managing desktops. In the bottom left of the screen, we also see the health, capacity, connection status, and number of active sessions. On the right, we see our familiar heatmaps broken up by the host at the top and virtual desktop at the bottom. As we know from earlier chapters, green means it's in good health, and red would be bad. The size of the blocks within the heatmaps is indicative of the size of the object. In the previous example, the hosts are the same size as are all the VMs.

The next dashboard we see is **View Users** as shown in the following screenshot:

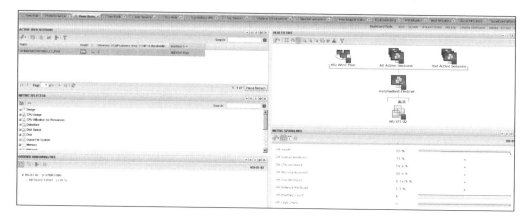

This dashboard shows us the users who are logged in and the desktops they're logged in to. We can select an object in **Health Tree** at the top right of the screen to see the metrics and anomalies associated with it on the left-hand side.

The Health Tree section also shows us the relationships of the virtual desktop to other View entities. At the bottom right, **Metric Sparklines** tells us things associated with Health, such as workload, faults, and anomalies.

We also have a **View Pools** tab that has some great information about the pool health.

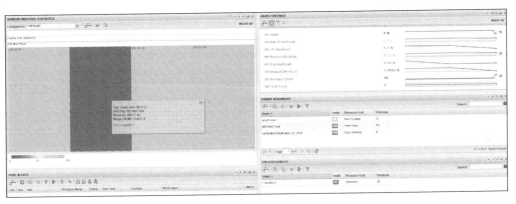

We see another heatmap on this page. Since there's only one pool, we only see one heatmap, which again shows the virtual desktops. When we click on one of the blocks within the heatmap, we're shown the health for that virtual desktop. We can also see the health of the host and the datastore it's associated with.

The **View Sessions** tab shown as follows gives us much of the same information configured in a way that is different to the **View Users** tab. We can also choose to look at things besides health, such as workload, latency, bandwidth, and packet loss. Things like bandwidth, storage performance, latency, and packet loss can be really interesting metrics to look at if our users are complaining of poor performance or issues such as that of a video not displaying properly.

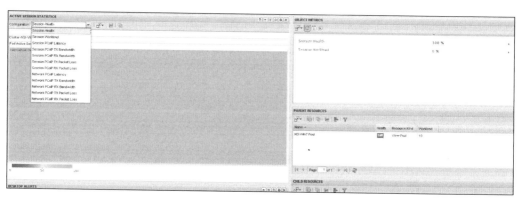

If we want to compare the pools based on utilization, health, workload, and so on, we can use the **Top Pools** tab available. There's a **Top Sessions** tab and a **Top Desktop VMs** tab to do the same; but they are sorted by sessions as well.

If we're looking for something more, such as the Environment dashboard in the regular UI, we can click on the **View Infrastructure** tab.

From this tab, we see the familiar skittles that represent objects within the View environment. They are color coded according to health, workload, anomalies, or faults scores. If we select one of the skittles, it highlights the other skittles that are associated with it. On the right, we can see graphs depending on the minor badge we've selected to view. It also shows us anomalous behavior via the small icon to the right of the graph and the abnormalities listed at the bottom right of the screen.

Finally, we have the **View Adapter** tab where we can see the connection status of the adapter and broker as well as more information on connected sessions.

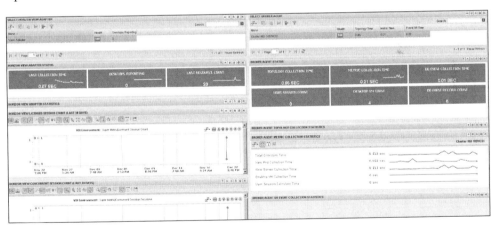

# Practical uses

As we saw in a few of the previous screenshots, there was one virtual desktop that was red within a few of the heatmaps. Let's explore that first. If we click on the **View Pools** tab and select **VM Health**, we see the red VM as shown in the following screenshot:

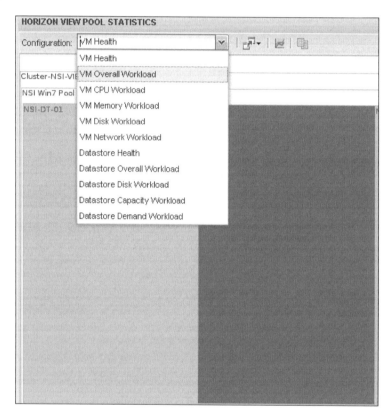

However, if we pick any of the other configurations, the heatmap is all green. So, it appears that the workload for that VM is fine. The CPU, memory, and datastore are all being utilized in an acceptable manner. If we look at the right-hand side under **Object Metrics**, though, we can see the anomalies score is really high. In fact, it's the only other score that's red.

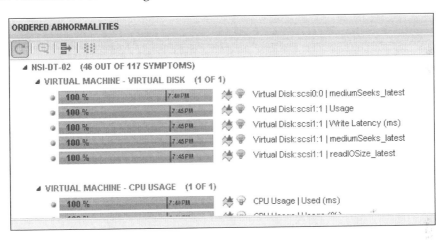

Then, if we click on the **View Infrastructure** tab, we can see the actual anomalies to explore whether it's something we need to be concerned about.

If we look at the **Virtual Disk** anomalies, we see that none of them are currently active because the little light bulb is clear or not lit up. Some of the CPU usage light bulbs are lit up, so they're active. However, we're not seeing any indication of overuse from the workload scores. Most likely this virtual desktop has been sitting idle for a while, and now that someone is logged into it, we're seeing some anomalous behavior. This will probably be corrected as we continue to learn the environment and gather more historical metrics.

To make sure that we can double-click on the red skittle representing the View desktop. This will let us drill in to the VM itself.

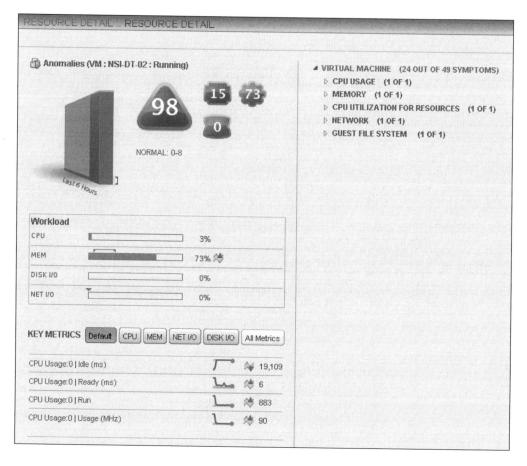

We're looking at the Workload badge because it's the only red minor badge. If we look under **Workload**, we can see that memory is a little high, but it's not out of memory yet. CPU, disk, and network are all really low.

We can also now search alerts for anything showing up in the View environment. If we hover over or double-click on the alerts in the upper-right corner, we see all of the alerts.

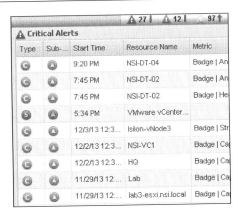

If we click on the alerts category at the top of the screen to see the Alerts Overview we can get a better view of the alerts in our environment, and we can even filter for events related to View in the tree on the left-hand side. Through the alerts, we'll be able to see all sorts of issues, such as login problems, pool provisioning problems, and overutilization of compute resources. Often, we'll see alerts before users even start to experience any performance issues.

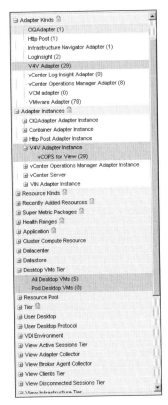

# Summary

We went through a high-level overview of the components that make up the View infrastructure. We have the connection server, security server, View desktops, and View pools among some other optional components.

We then went on to install vC OPS for the View adapter and the broker agent. These are the only components necessary for View 5.2 and above to begin collecting data. Once that was installed, we were able to go through the View dashboards that were created automatically. Through the use of these dashboards that we have customized, we can get an in-depth look at our View environment. Since vC OPS is able to learn "normal behavior", we can also get a look at historical data and anomalies.

In the next chapter, we'll go through vCenter Infrastructure Navigator. As noted earlier in this book, Infrastructure Navigator is a part of the vCenter Operations Manager Suite. We'll get it installed and working with vC OPS and then look at some practical uses for it.

# 10
# vCenter Infrastructure Navigator

Infrastructure Navigator is a part of the vCenter Operations Manager Suite Advanced edition and above. Something lacking in vCenter and vC OPS is the ability to automatically map and monitor applications and dependent services. Infrastructure Navigator does just that. It's essentially a plugin to vCenter, but comes along with an embedded adapter in vC OPS. We can actually monitor VMs that belong to critical applications and automatically group them within vC OPS for ease of use.

In this chapter, we'll cover the following topics:

- High-level overview of Infrastructure Navigator
- How to connect vC OPS with Infrastructure Navigator
- Practical uses

# Overview of Infrastructure Navigator

Infrastructure Navigator is a downloadable virtual appliance. It comes with a built-in database and offers a plugin to be used with the vSphere Client. To begin, we'll deploy the Infrastructure Navigator OVA template we downloaded from VMware in the same way we did for VCM in *Chapter 7, vCenter Configuration Manager*. We'll specify the network information for the VM as shown in the following screenshot:

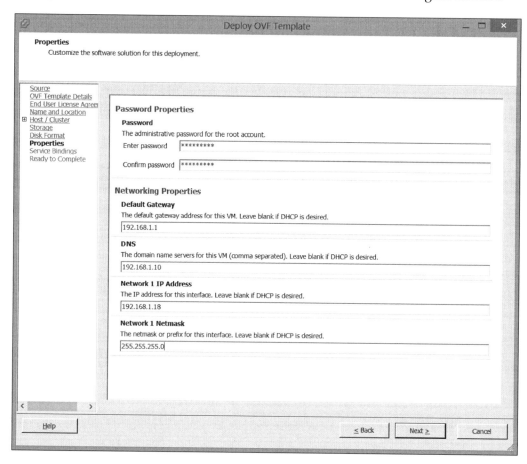

We also need to specify a service binding so that Infrastructure Navigator, or VIN, has access to everything from vCenter.

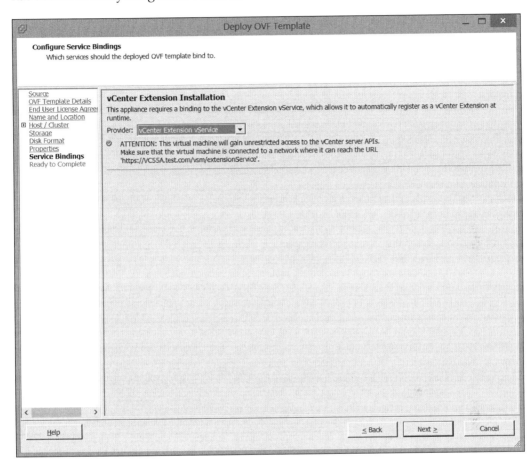

If we're using vCenter 5.1 and above, this is all the configuration that needs to be done. If we're using 5.0 or below, there are some other configurations that need to be made. Now if we open our web client, we'll see an **Infrastructure Navigator** tab on the left-hand side. Click on the **Infrastructure Navigator** tab to change the settings.

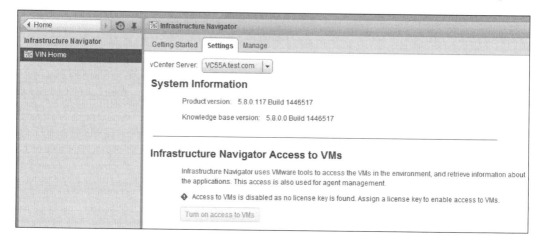

To enable access to VMs, we need to be sure to license VIN. VIN can be licensed through the licensing UI on the vSphere web client. After we license it, we can click on the **Turn on access to VMs** button. We need to enter our vCenter username and password in the pop up. Once we've turned on access to the VMs, we can create rules under the **Manage** tab. We want to create these rules to collect information on which VMs are part of a certain application. These automated rules define the patterns that we're looking for from certain VMs and automatically put them into a collection of VMs that belong to an application or service. Though we can create manual rules and still use VIN, the automated rules certainly add some ease of use as well as provide a starting point. On the left, we select the **Service Category** and on the right, we select the **Service Name** within that category. The following screenshot shows a Database Server on the left and the options we have for the Database Server on the right.

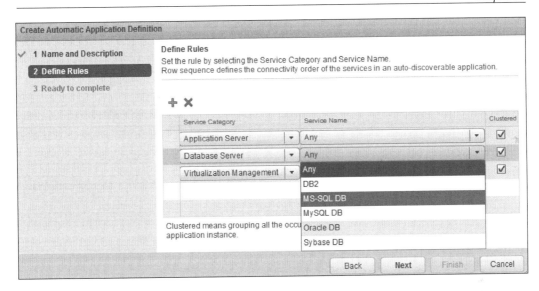

We can also choose **Any** from the drop-down menu and **Other** for any proprietary or in-house type of application servers. Now that we have everything configured, we can click on any VM and see the **Infrastructure Navigator** pane within the **Summary** tab. In the following screenshot, the vCenter VM is selected and we see that it has eight dependencies:

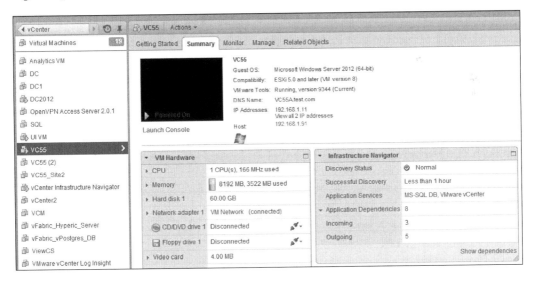

We can then click on the **Show dependencies** link that takes us to the **Application Dependencies** tab for the VM we've clicked on. Here we get a map of the services and other servers this VM is connected to. We can also change it to **Table View** depending on how we want it to look. We could manually note the dependencies and begin looking for things based on what we've found through VIN, but there's an easier way to integrate with vC OPS, which we'll go over in the next section.

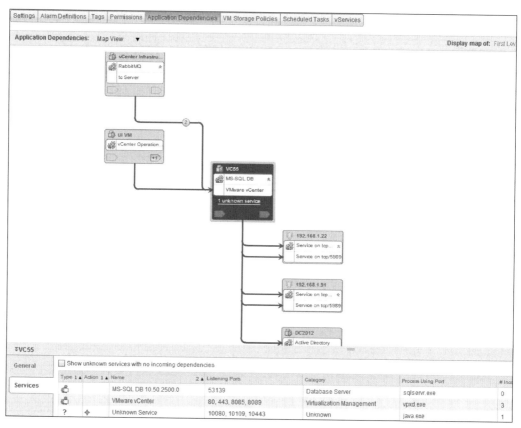

# Using VIN with vC OPS

Unlike the View adapter, the VIN adapter is built in as long as you're running at least vC OPS Advanced. Since we've already connected VIN to vCenter using the web client, we're actually all set from an installation perspective. However, there are some things we need to set up in order for vC OPS to automatically report on the mappings VIN has discovered.

To begin, we'll select a VM in the web client. In the following steps, we'll use one of the View Connection Servers, but it could really be anything. We could do this with an SQL server, ADD servers, or any grouping we'd like to make.

1. Click on the **ViewCS1** VM in the vSphere web client.

2. Click on the **Manage** tab.

3. Click on **Application Dependencies**. First we see that it's displaying a map of **First Level Of Dependencies**.

4. Click on the icon right next to it to **Create Application**.

5. Call the application something. In this case, we'll call it `View`.

6. Next to **Display map of:**, click on the drop-down arrow and change it to **View** (or whatever we named the application in the previous step).

7. Now we only see the connection server for this display map. If we click on the arrow at the bottom left of this VM, we see mapping to other VMs. We use *Ctrl* + right-click to highlight whichever VMs and services we want to include in this group. For instance, we might select other connection servers or security servers we'd like to include.

8. Once we've highlighted the other VMs and services, we can click on the **Add selected application members** icon to include them in the group as shown in the following screenshot.

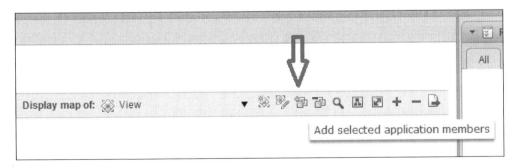

From the web-client side, that's all we need to do. We can create as many of these groups or mappings as we like. Servers can be in several different groups. For instance, we may have a SQL server group, but our SQL servers may be in several other application groups as well.

We can now log into the vC OPS UI. These new groups will be reflected under the **Groups** category within **Application**. If we looked at the **Groups** category before, we would not see an **Application** section. We must create the groups as we did in the previous steps for this to work, but it will automatically create the group. It may also take several minutes for it to appear.

As the previous screenshot shows, we can see the major badges as well as any minor badges for this entire group. If someone is complaining about a View desktop being slow, we can click on the **View Application** group to find out if there are any VMs within the group that appear in red. Perhaps a better example of this would be if we created a group for a proprietary application we've created in-house. There are several database servers, applications servers, and web servers associated with the application. We might be able to see that the application server is running fine, but without VIN and vC OPS it's going to take us a lot longer to narrow down where the performance issue is coming from. This gives us one place to check. Also, with VIN, we might see dependent services we didn't even know were associated with the application.

We can also see interesting metrics from the other tabs and for the entire group at the same time. For instance, the **Operations** tab shows us any metric we could possibly want to see.

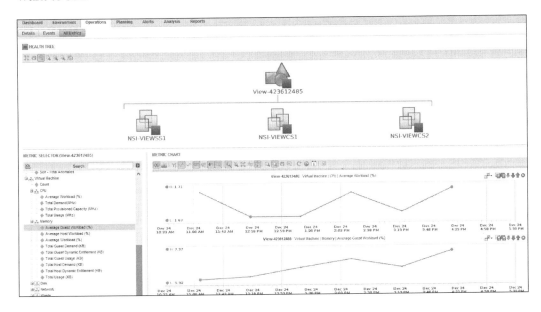

Unfortunately, we're not able to create a what-if scenario for the application group. It would be interesting to perform some capacity planning using the what-if scenarios based on the application. However, we do have many of the Views available under the **Planning** tab for some manual capacity planning.

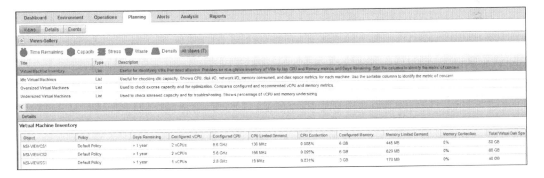

# Summary

Although VIN is definitely a niche product, it would be an asset to any large company. It integrates with both VMware Site Recovery Manager as well as vCenter Operations. We saw how it will automatically discover mappings and dependent services to show relationships of VMs. We can also create mappings that will then be put into the vC OPS interface automatically. From the vC OPS interface, we can monitor an entire application, taking away the guesswork of an administrator.

In the next and last chapter, we'll go over how we can use vCenter Operations to monitor an EMC VNX. This will give us many more details on storage than we had without using the EMC Storage Analytics management pack.

# 11
# EMC Storage Analytics

**Management packs** are add-ons from different vendors for vCenter Operations Manager. There are several add-ons available on the VMware Solution Exchange site (`https://solutionexchange.vmware.com/store`), which any customer can access for free after creating an account. There are management packs from Microsoft for Active Directory and SQL information, NetApp for storage information on NetApp devices, and EMC for storage information on EMC arrays. In this chapter, we'll go through deploying the EMC Storage Analytics management pack, which we can use to get more detailed metrics for the CX and VNX series of EMC arrays.

We'll cover the following topics in this chapter:

- Deploying the **EMC Storage Analytics (ESA)** management pack
- Using ESA with vC OPS

## Deploying ESA

We can download ESA from either VMware Solution Exchange or from EMC. They are the same product. It comes as a `.pak` file, which we've seen earlier in this book. Once we have that downloaded, we can get started using the following steps:

1. Login to the vC OPS admin console at `https://<vCOPS_IP_Address>/admin`.
2. Click on the **Update** tab.
3. Click on **Browse** and click on the ESA `.pak` file we've downloaded to update vC OPS with ESA.
4. Click on **Update**.

5.  Accept the EULA and wait for the update to complete.

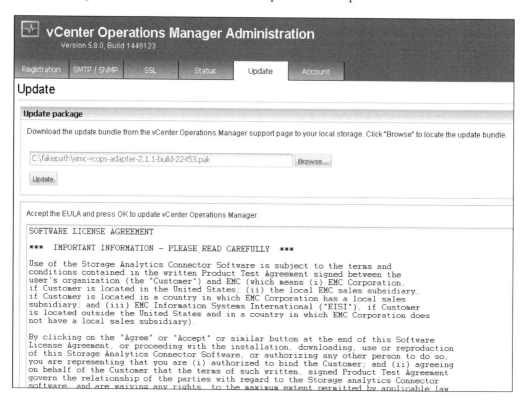

6.  We now need to log in to the custom UI available in the enterprise version by going to `https://<vCOPS_IP_address>/vcops-custom`. Now, hover over **Environment**, then go to **Configuration** and click on **Adapter Instances...**.

7.  Click on the **Add a new adapter instance** icon.

8.  For **Collector**, select your vCenter Operations server or whichever collector you'd like to use.

9.  For **Adapter Kind**, select **EMC Adapter**.

10. Now we can fill out the rest of the information so it connects to our VNX in this case. We'll most likely need to add credentials. For this, we'll use password credentials and then the username and password we use to connect to the VNX.

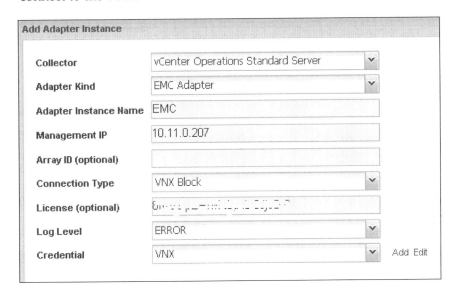

11. Click on **Test**.

12. Check that everything tests successfully. If it's not successful, check that you have the proper **Management IP** and that there are no firewalls blocking the connection.

13. Click on **Apply** and **OK**.

This completes the installation and configuration of the ESA adapter. Once we've completed installing vC OPS, it will start collecting data from our VNX.

We can actually use ESA even if we don't have the enterprise versions of vC OPS. There is an OEM version of vC OPS that we can download from EMC. We won't get all the perks of vC OPS using this, but we can still use it to monitor and analyze EMC arrays. We need to purchase the Storage Analytics Suite from EMC to get it all licensed.

# Using ESA with vC OPS

If we log back in to the vC OPS custom UI, we see that we have a lot of dashboards pertaining to EMC as shown in the following screenshot:

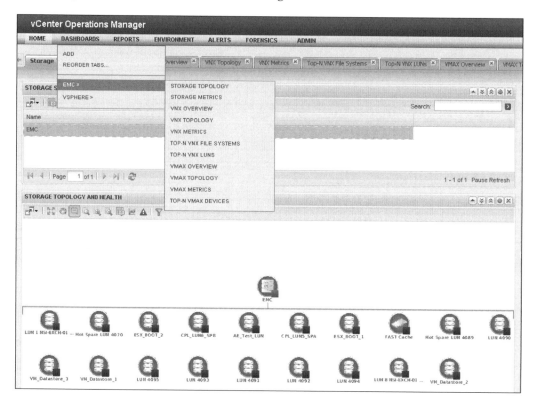

The previous screenshot shows **STORAGE TOPOLOGY**, which is a kind of general tab. We see the various LUNs we have carved up as well as their health. The top level shows in green, which is good, and the rest are in blue, which means it's still collecting information. To the right of the **STORAGE TOPOLOGY** dashboard, we see more detailed information about everything from disk to LUN.

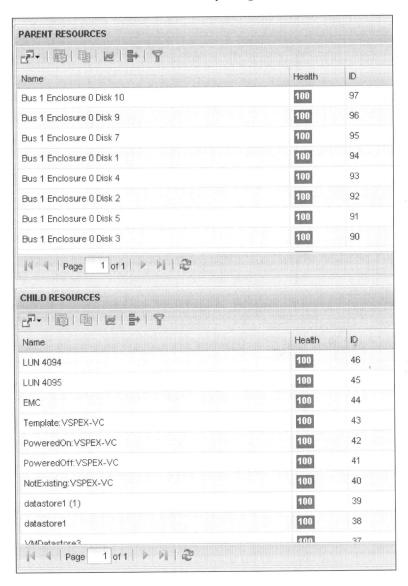

If we look at the next dashboard, we can see **STORAGE METRICS**. This gives us more data that is specific to our array such as auto-tiered information, performance metrics for storage processors, trespasses, and capacity information.

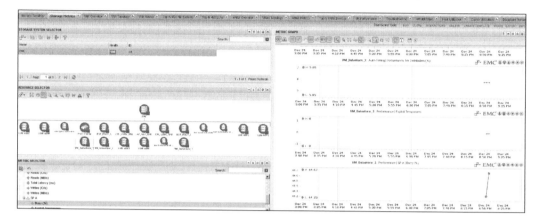

Our **VNX Overview** dashboard is filled with heatmaps that give us health information for storage processors or data movers depending on whether you're using a block of file level storage. We can see capacity information, cache performance, and LUN and file performance. As we can see in the following screenshot, the **Write Cache Hit Ratio** is in red. This means we're probably not seeing a lot of use out of our cache tier. In a production environment, this would be worrisome—after all, we've probably paid a lot of money for the flash drives. In the environment shown in the following screenshot, we're probably seeing it because it's a lab that isn't doing much:

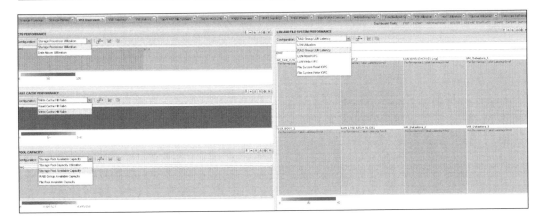

The next dashboard we specifically see is **VNX Topology**. This dashboard is reminiscent of the regular UI where we can see skittles and their health based on the color. However, we see many array-related categories such as RAID groups, storage processors, tiers, and disks. We can click on the skittles to see which other components they have dependencies with. On the right-hand side, we see the **Health Tree** related to the skittle we've selected as well as the **METRIC SPARKLINES** dashboard related to it as shown in the following screenshot:

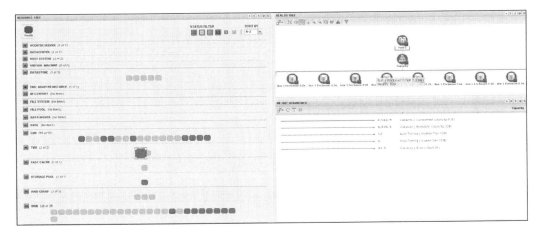

We have another VNX-specific dashboard that shows us the same **Resource Tree** to the left called **VNX Metrics**. To the right, we can see specific metrics for any object we choose in the **Resource Tree**.

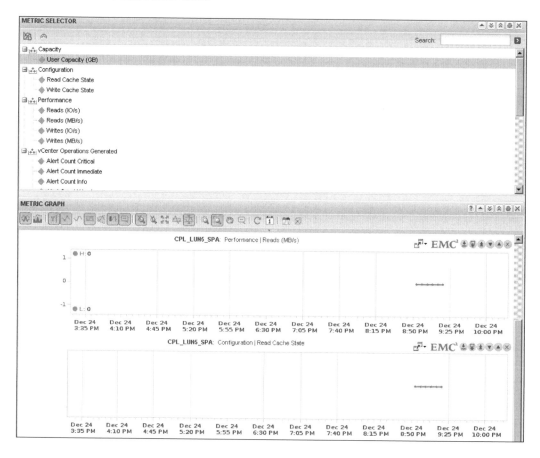

The last graph shown here is the **Top-N VNX LUNs**. This shows several graphs based on the top LUN utilization and capacity. This could help with data distribution within our storage array or to get a general idea of the utilization and capacity within our environment.

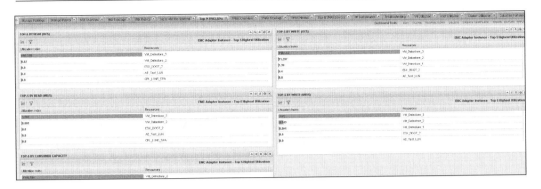

There are some other dashboards available. We can see the top DataMover information if we are using file-level storage. We also have several dashboards pertaining to VMAX. These dashboards are very similar to the ones shown in the previous screenshot but specific to the VMAX, another EMC storage product. As always with the custom UI, we can also create our own dashboards with the widgets now available from the EMC dashboards.

# Summary

In this chapter, we went through the deployment of the EMC Storage Analytics management pack available from the EMC site as well as VMware Solution Exchange. This management pack gives us more detailed information of components within our storage arrays that vC OPS itself does not have access to.

There are many management packs and add-ins available from other vendors as well as VMware for vC OPS. Many of them are deployed in the same way as the previous chapters have shown but give you information specifically for that vendor's product.

# Index

## Symbols

## A

## B

## C

## D

## N

**navigation overview**
about 40
Alerts tab 48
Analysis tab 48
Dashboard tab 41
Environment tab 41-43
Operations tab 44, 45
Planning tab 46, 47
Reports tab 49
**network performance**
troubleshooting 88, 89
**network protocol profiles 19**

## O

**Operations tab 44, 45**
**Oversized Virtual Machines report 134, 135**

## P

**Performance Correlation report 142**
**persistent disks 189**
**Planning tab 46, 47**
**pod 198**
**policies, vC Ops Manager**
managing 31
**pools 189**

## R

**Reclaimable Waste badge 59**
**Reports tab 49**
**resources, vC Ops custom dashboard**
adding 36, 37
**Risk badge 52**

## S

**Security Information and Event Management (SIEM) 169**
**slow applications**
troubleshooting 89, 90
**Solution Exchange**
URL 217
**Stress badge 58, 59**

## T

**tag**
creating 64, 65
**ThinApps 189**
**Time Remaining badge 56, 57**
**troubleshooting, virtual environment**
about 67
future risks, searching 91-93
major badges, drilling in 68-77
minor badges, drilling in 68-77
network performance, troubleshooting 88, 89
slow applications, troubleshooting 89, 90
VM performance, troubleshooting 78-87
**troubleshooting, with vC Ops**
benefits 10

## U

**UI VM 19**
**user permissions, vC Ops custom dashboard**
configuring 35

## V

**vCenter Configuration Manager (VCM)**
about 145
installing 145-148
**vCenter Operations Manager.** *See* **vC Ops**
**vC Ops Manager configuration**
display settings, managing 32
group types, managing 32
licenses, assigning 29, 30
performing 25-28
policies, managing 31
**vC Ops Manager Standalone 19**
**vC Ops Manager Suite**
about 14, 207
components 14
**vCenter Server**
IP pool, configuring 20, 21
preparing 18, 19
**VCM**
basic configuration 149-154
connecting, to vC Ops 155-162

## Thank you for buying
## VMware vCenter Operations Manager Essentials

# About Packt Publishing

Packt, pronounced 'packed', published its first book "Mastering phpMyAdmin for Effective MySQL Management" in April 2004 and subsequently continued to specialize in publishing highly focused books on specific technologies and solutions.

Our books and publications share the experiences of your fellow IT professionals in adapting and customizing today's systems, applications, and frameworks. Our solution based books give you the knowledge and power to customize the software and technologies you're using to get the job done. Packt books are more specific and less general than the IT books you have seen in the past. Our unique business model allows us to bring you more focused information, giving you more of what you need to know, and less of what you don't.

Packt is a modern, yet unique publishing company, which focuses on producing quality, cutting-edge books for communities of developers, administrators, and newbies alike. For more information, please visit our website: www.packtpub.com.

# About Packt Enterprise

In 2010, Packt launched two new brands, Packt Enterprise and Packt Open Source, in order to continue its focus on specialization. This book is part of the Packt Enterprise brand, home to books published on enterprise software – software created by major vendors, including (but not limited to) IBM, Microsoft and Oracle, often for use in other corporations. Its titles will offer information relevant to a range of users of this software, including administrators, developers, architects, and end users.

# Writing for Packt

We welcome all inquiries from people who are interested in authoring. Book proposals should be sent to author@packtpub.com. If your book idea is still at an early stage and you would like to discuss it first before writing a formal book proposal, contact us; one of our commissioning editors will get in touch with you.

We're not just looking for published authors; if you have strong technical skills but no writing experience, our experienced editors can help you develop a writing career, or simply get some additional reward for your expertise.

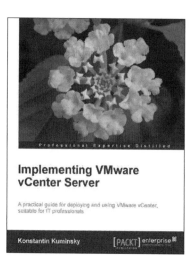

## Implementing VMware vCenter Server

ISBN: 978-1-84968-998-4          Paperback: 324 pages

A practical guide for deploying and using VMware vCenter, suitable for IT professionals

1. Gain in-depth knowledge of the VMware vCenter features, requirements, and deployment process

2. Manage hosts, virtual machines, and learn storage management in VMware vCenter server

3. Overview of VMware vCenter Operations Manager and VMware vCenter Orchestrator

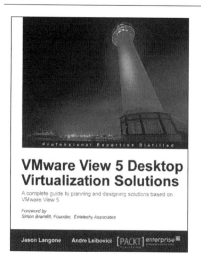

## VMware View 5 Desktop Virtualization Solutions

ISBN: 978-1-84968-112-4          Paperback: 288 pages

A complete guide to planning and designing solutions based on VMware View 5

1. Written by VMware experts Jason Langone and Andre Leibovici, this book is a complete guide to planning and designing a solution based on VMware View 5

2. Secure your Visual Desktop Infrastructure (VDI) by having firewalls, antivirus, virtual enclaves, USB redirection and filtering and smart card authentication

3. Analyze the strategies and techniques used to migrate a user population from a physical desktop environment to a virtual desktop solution

Please check **www.PacktPub.com** for information on our titles

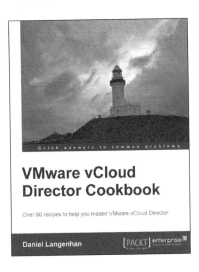

## VMware vCloud Director Cookbook

ISBN: 978-1-78217-766-1     Paperback: 364 pages

Over 80 recipes to help you master VMware vCloud Director

1. Learn how to work with the vCloud API

2. Covers the recently launched VMware vCloud Suite 5.5

3. Step-by-step instructions to simplify infrastructure provisioning

4. Real-life implementation of tested recipes, packed with illustrations and programming examples

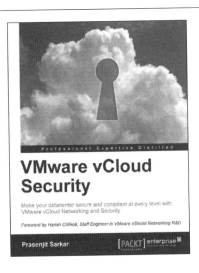

## VMware vCloud Security

ISBN: 978-1-78217-096-9     Paperback: 106 pages

Make your datacenter secure and complaint at every level with VMware vCloud Networking and Security

1. Take away an in-depth knowledge of how to secure a private cloud running on vCloud Director

2. Enable the reader with the knowledge, skills, and abilities to achieve competence at building and running a secured private cloud

3. Focuses on giving you broader view of the security and compliance while still being manageable and flexible to scale

Please check **www.PacktPub.com** for information on our titles